Jennifer Lopez

Titles in the People in the News series include:

PEOPLE
IN THE NEWS

Jennifer Lopez

by Heidi Hurst

LUCENT BOOKS®

THOMSON

GALE

San Diego • Detroit • New York • San Francisco • Cleveland
New Haven, Conn. • Waterville, Maine • London • Munich

Thank you to my parents, brother, and sister, and my posse of aunts, uncles, and cousins who provide endless love and support.

LIBRARY OF CONGRESS CATALOGING-IN-PUBLICATION DATA

Hurst, Heidi.
    Jennifer Lopez / by Heidi Hurst.
        p. cm. — (People in the news)
Summary: A biography of Jennifer Lopez, whose talent and determination have led to her success as an actress, singer, and dancer.
    Includes bibliographical references (p.) and index.
    ISBN 1-59018-325-8 (hardback : alk. paper)
    1. Lopez, Jennifer, 1970—Juvenile literature. 2. Singers—United States—Biography—Juvenile literature. [1. Lopez, Jennifer, 1970 – 2. Actors and actresses. 3. Singers—United States— Biography—Juvenile literature – 4. Women—Biography. 5. Hispanic Americans — Biography] I. Title.
    PN2287.L634H87 2004
    791.43′028′092—dc21

                                      2003007444

Printed in the United States of America

Table of Contents

Foreword

FAME AND CELEBRITY are alluring. People are drawn to those who walk in fame's spotlight, whether they are known for great accomplishments or for notorious deeds. The lives of the famous pique public interest and attract attention, perhaps because their experiences seem in some ways so different from, yet in other ways so similar to, our own.

Newspapers, magazines, and television regularly capitalize on this fascination with celebrity by running profiles of famous people. For example, television programs such as *Entertainment Tonight* devote all of their programming to stories about entertainment and entertainers. Magazines such as *People* fill their pages with stories of the private lives of famous people. Even newspapers, newsmagazines, and television news frequently delve into the lives of well-known personalities. Despite the number of articles and programs, few provide more than a superficial glimpse at their subjects.

Lucent's People in the News series offers young readers a deeper look into the lives of today's newsmakers, the influences that have shaped them, and the impact they have had in their fields of endeavor and on other people's lives. The subjects of the series hail from many disciplines and walks of life. They include authors, musicians, athletes, political leaders, entertainers, entrepreneurs, and others who have made a mark on modern life and who, in many cases, will continue to do so for years to come.

These biographies are more than factual chronicles. Each book emphasizes the contributions, accomplishments, or deeds that have brought fame or notoriety to the individual and shows how that person has influenced modern life. Authors portray their subjects in a realistic, unsentimental light. For example, Bill Gates—the cofounder and chief executive officer of the software giant Microsoft—has been instrumental in making personal computers the most vital tool of the modern age. Few dispute his business savvy, his perseverance, or his technical expertise, yet critics say he is ruthless in his dealings with competitors and driven more by his desire to maintain Microsoft's dominance in the computer industry than by an interest in furthering technology.

In these books, young readers will encounter inspiring stories about real people who achieved success despite enormous obstacles. Oprah Winfrey—the most powerful, most watched, and wealthiest woman on television today—spent the first six years of her life in the care of her grandparents while her unwed mother sought work and a better life elsewhere. Her adolescence was colored by promiscuity, pregnancy at age fourteen, rape, and sexual abuse.

Each author documents and supports his or her work with an array of primary and secondary source quotations taken from diaries, letters, speeches, and interviews. All quotes are footnoted to show readers exactly how and where biographers derive their information and provide guidance for further research. The quotations enliven the text by giving readers eyewitness views of the life and accomplishments of each person covered in the People in the News series.

In addition, each book in the series includes photographs, annotated bibliographies, timelines, and comprehensive indexes. For both the casual reader and the student researcher, the People in the News series offers insight into the lives of today's newsmakers—people who shape the way we live, work, and play in the modern age.

Introduction

A Girl with a Dream

As A CHILD IN THE MID-1970s, Jennifer Lopez watched movies and dreamed of being a part of them. However, these were pipe dreams for Latinos at this time; very few Latino actors or performers had achieved celebrity status when young Jennifer was growing up. But Lopez did not mind the challenge. She hoped to break down the barriers for Latinos in the entertainment business and prove that when it came to success, it was not about heritage. It was about talent. It was her dream and her commitment that took her from a little girl in Bronx, New York, to becoming one of the world's biggest superstars.

The Beginning

As a Latin girl in the Bronx, Lopez excelled in dance classes and told anyone who would listen that she was going to be a star. In her community, however, she was laughed at. Neighbors told her a Latino could never be such a huge star. Worried for her future, her parents encouraged Lopez to attend college, become a lawyer, and forget her show business dreams. At age eighteen, after years of dance lessons and auditions, Lopez made her parents proud when she enrolled in Baruch College. However, after a year she dropped out because her heart was in performing. Leaving home for the big city of Manhattan, Lopez vowed to work until she achieved her dream. She dreamed of acting, but used her dance career to get her to Hollywood.

After landing a spot as a Fly Girl on the Fox television comedy show *In Living Color*, Lopez moved to Hollywood with stars in her eyes. With sheer determination and confidence, Lopez pursued an acting career while dancing. Her hard work paid off when she was cast in television sitcoms and then made the transition to films. A few high-profile films later, Lopez was one of Hollywood's brightest stars. Now, she is the highest-paid Latina actress in the world, a title of which she is proud.

Never Enough

Lopez had come from small beginnings to the top of Hollywood's A-list, but it was not enough. A self-proclaimed perfectionist, she refused to stop working until she pursued every dream. A goal of recording an album led to four No. 1 albums and a successful music career. Lopez had achieved her performing goals, but she wanted more. A clothing line, a restaurant, and a fragrance followed, but that still did not bring complete satisfaction. No matter how successful she had become, in the back of her mind, Lopez could still hear the voices of those in her neighborhood who doubted her. In an effort to prove them wrong, she continued to work hard. On the outside she seemed a true success, but on the inside she was not completely happy.

Dreaming of stardom since childhood, Jennifer Lopez is today the most successful Latina actress in the world.

Professionally, Lopez had achieved feats beyond her wildest dreams. The nonstop work, however, had begun to take its toll. Two marriages and two long-term relationships fell victim to her busy schedule. She was lonely and often worried that she would never find her true soul mate. But maintaining her success was a full-time commitment.

Falling in Love

In 2002, Lopez was on top of the world. She was a role model, sex symbol, and celebrity icon. She made weekly appearances on the covers of tabloid magazines. Her fans and the public in general just could not get enough. Whether it was her latest rumored love or another example of her supposed divalike behavior, Lopez was a media darling. By now, Lopez was considered a superstar not because of her heritage but because of her personality. She had broken down the ethnic barriers, and professionally, she could have the world.

What the confessed romantic really wanted, however, was to fall deeply in love and have a long, successful marriage. When she met actor Ben Affleck, she saw that dream coming true. Together, Lopez and Affleck became the most talked about couple in the country. The world became just as interested in their relationship as they had.

At the dawn of the twenty-first century, Lopez has the future in her hands, and she is taking advantage of it. With a slew of films to star in, including one that will possibly bring her a much coveted Academy Award, Lopez's achievements are a dream come true. Her biggest production, however, will be when she and Affleck begin a family. To Lopez, her Hollywood success will be nothing compared to the love of a family. Whether Lopez can make this relationship last or whether it will go the way of her past failed loves, she can be sure the public will not lose interest in her inspiring life story.

Chapter 1

Destined for Stardom

JENNIFER LOPEZ WAS BORN to be a star. At least that is what she has believed since she was a child. Born on July 24, 1970, in Bronx, New York, Jennifer Lynn Lopez was brought up in a loving Puerto Rican family. The middle of three daughters, Jennifer was dedicated to pleasing her parents, David and Guadalupe. With their support, Jennifer was brought up with confidence and willpower that would take her farther than she ever imagined.

David and Guadalupe Lopez both hailed from the same town in Puerto Rico. However, they did not meet until their youth, when their families moved to New York City. Thanks to their similar backgrounds, David and Guadalupe fell in love. The couple married and bought a home in the Castle Hill neighborhood of the Bronx. Although the Bronx had a reputation for crime, the Lopez house was in a safe neighborhood. However, even as close as a few blocks away, it was unsafe to be out alone at night. "It wasn't so much a bad neighborhood as one where you had to be careful," Jennifer said. "The sensibilities you grow up with in a city teach you to be more alert, aware, more careful."[1] David became a computer specialist for Guardian Insurance in Manhattan, while Guadalupe earned money as a schoolteacher in Westchester County, New York. David and Guadalupe both worked hard to provide a comfortable living for their family, which included Jennifer's older sister, Leslie, and her younger sister, Lynda.

The Lopez daughters had a happy childhood, even though their parents could not afford to spoil them. There were times when the girls would have to wear old clothes or shoes while their friends had nicer outfits. Jennifer was embarrassed to have holes in her shoes, and at times she yearned for the nicer things in life. But she knew all that really mattered was that her family was loving and healthy.

Jennifer's Spark

The typical middle child, Jennifer yearned for her parents' sole attention. Early on, she showed a knack for performing and she would put on shows for her family in their living room. At age five, her parents enrolled her in dance classes at the local Kips Bay Boys & Girls Club. She learned ballet and jazz dancing. She immediately fell in love with dancing. Jennifer could not wait to show her parents the routines she had learned. Even though she

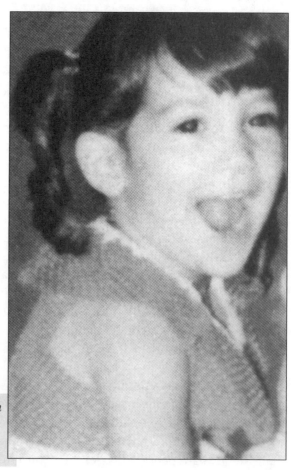

Jennifer was born in New York in 1970. She is the second of three children.

was very young, Jennifer knew that she wanted to perform for the rest of her life. Along with dance lessons, young Jennifer was enrolled in piano lessons, and she liked to sing. Music was always part of the Lopez household: Guadalupe loved current R&B music and David played a lot of Latin music as well. The Lopez girls were always aware and proud of their Latin heritage.

Jennifer's hero was Latin, too. Her childhood idol was actress and dancer Rita Moreno. Moreno starred in Jennifer's favorite movie, *West Side Story*. She played Anita, the girlfriend of Bernardo, head of a Puerto Rican gang in 1950s New York. Bernardo's gang, the Sharks, were enemies of a white gang, the Jets. However, the plot took an even more dramatic turn when Bernardo's sister, Maria, fell in love with Jet Tony. Their love ends in tragedy, however, as Tony was killed in a fight. Although the tragic story line was a little over her head, the young Jennifer adored the singing and dancing in the film. She also felt proud to see a Latina actress playing in such a glamorous movie. Watching Rita Moreno in *West Side Story*, Jennifer thought it might be fun to be an actress who sings and dances, too. After watching the movie, she and her sisters acted out scenes from the film for their mother. Guadalupe noticed that Jennifer was a natural performer, but she was cautious about encouraging her. She knew her daughter had what it took to be a star, but knowing the limitations for Latinos in Hollywood at the time, she thought it best not to push Jennifer into pursuing entertainment full time. She wanted to protect her daughter from heartbreak and rejection.

The Lopez Work Ethic

While instilling pride of their Latin heritage in their daughters, David and Guadalupe also promoted a strict work ethic. No one in the family was to miss a day of work, church, or school. Jennifer and her sisters attended Holy Family Catholic School. David and Guadalupe were proud to give their daughters a private school education, even if it meant they would have to work extra hours. David often worked late nights and sacrificed time with his daughters just to provide for his family. Jennifer

Rita Moreno

As a child, Jennifer Lopez watched Rita Moreno in *West Side Story* and dreamed of becoming an actress just like her. The actresses actually have a lot in common. Rita Moreno was born Rosa Dolores Alverio on December 11, 1932, in Humacao, Puerto Rico. After her family moved to New York when she was a child, she began to take dance lessons. At age thirteen, she made her Broadway debut as a dancer. In her later teens, she dreamed of a role in films. After meeting with famed MGM president Louis Mayer, he convinced her to change her name. She chose Rita Moreno. She played a series of forgettable roles until she was cast as Anita in the movie musical *West Side Story*. The 1961 film was a retelling of *Romeo and Juliet*, set on the streets of New York City. The film was a smash hit, and in 1962, Moreno won an Academy Award for her role. After receiving the award, Moreno donated one thousand dollars toward an acting scholarship at the University of Puerto Rico to help other young people with similar dreams. To this day, Moreno continues to act in film, television, and theater. Most recently she appeared in the HBO series *Oz*.

Rita Moreno (center, right) dances in a scene from West Side Story. *Moreno won an Academy Award for her work in the film.*

cherished spending every spare moment with her father. Even as a child, Jennifer appreciated her father's hard work. He became her role model and hero.

Jennifer especially loved the days she and her sisters were able to visit her father in Manhattan for lunch. Guadalupe would dress the girls up and they would ride the subway to downtown Manhattan to meet David at his office. As a family, they went out to eat or brought a picnic lunch and walked around the city. Although they lived just a subway ride away, the big city was still unfamiliar to Jennifer, who spent much of her time around home. But there was something about being in the city, with the excitement of the crowds and the views of the tall buildings, that inspired Jennifer. This was a world she did not know, but she knew she wanted to be a part of it. Manhattan was glamorous to Jennifer, plus it was home to Broadway. Jennifer dreamed of being in a Broadway musical one day, so she could sing and dance just like Rita Moreno.

Her New Loves

When Jennifer was nine, the first rap song to receive national airplay became popular. "Rappers Delight" by the Sugarhill Gang was a huge success. Jennifer loved the song, especially since the rap group came from the Bronx, too. She liked to dance to the song because of its funky beats and new sound. Hearing the song on the radio, she realized that even people from her neighborhood could become famous. The new sound of rap quickly became one of Jennifer's favorite types of music.

However, as a preteen, Jennifer also discovered Madonna. The '80s pop icon was controversial, brash, and flamboyant, and Jennifer adored her. Before Madonna came along, Jennifer was a jeans and T-shirt kind of girl. When Madonna flaunted her own unique fashion sense, Jennifer was captivated and began to experiment with her own style. Under Madonna's influence, Lopez went from tomboy to fashion conscious overnight. Madonna quickly became another role model to Jennifer. Although she had admired Rita Moreno for her similar heritage and talent, she adored Madonna for her pop music and flashiness. Watching

Friend for Life

As a young child, Jennifer Lopez met her best friend for life: Arlene Rodriguez. Both students at Holy Family Catholic School in the Bronx, Rodriguez retold the story of the first time they met in a January 2001 interview with *Seventeen* titled "Livin' La Vida Lopez." "Jennifer kicked me, and then we became friends," she said. "Jennifer thought she was going to take over the place. She had all these friends and she was like, 'You get my shoes, you get this, you get that.' I saw everybody running and getting her stuff, and I said, 'No!' So she came up and kicked me in the knee. I told on her and she got in trouble."

After their initial meeting, Lopez and Rodriguez became inseparable, even sneaking out of their homes to attend a Menudo concert in middle school. Rodriguez remained close to Lopez throughout her rise to fame, and in 1995, she moved to Los Angeles to become Lopez's personal assistant. Although Rodriguez resigned as her assistant in 2002 to pursue acting, Lopez continued to adore her friend. "You want to fit in, you want to be seen with the popular cool crowd," Lopez told *Seventeen* interviewer Laura Morgan. "But at the end of the day, you're going to walk away with one friend. For me, that friend is Arlene."

Madonna enjoy her status as a performer, Jennifer knew being an entertainer was in her future.

At age fifteen, Jennifer fell in love for the first time with local boy David Cruz. Since Jennifer was a pretty girl with an athletic dancer's body, she was attractive to many boys. Her mother worried that she was growing up too fast. She especially worried that Jennifer and David were progressing too fast with their relationship. Jennifer had worked too hard, she believed, to end up as a young mother. Even though Jennifer was careful, she often snuck out of the house to spend time with David. "I was always climbing out of windows, jumping off roofs and he was sneaking up. It was crazy,"[2] Jennifer said.

Her actions were out of character for the polite, respectful daddy's girl, but Jennifer was in love. She got caught up in the emotions and excitement of a new relationship. The newness did not wear off. Still, Jennifer had no intentions of marrying young and starting a family. She had an independent spirit and an iron will. Love was important, but pursuing her dreams meant even more.

Proving Them Wrong

Jennifer believed in her dreams, and her parents believed in her, but others in her neighborhood were not so optimistic. The teachers at Kips Bay Boys & Girls Club knew Jennifer had a spark and they encouraged her, but others in her neighborhood mocked her goal of becoming a star. They would tell her that a Latina like her could never be a glamorous celebrity. "When I said I wanted to be a performer, people went 'Yeah, right,'" Jennifer said. "You don't do that where I come from."[3] Jennifer refused to listen to naysayers. If anyone was going to succeed from her neighborhood, she truly felt like it would be her.

Madonna became an early role model for Jennifer Lopez. As an adolescent, Lopez admired the pop star's music and flashy sense of style.

At age sixteen, Jennifer auditioned for a role in the film *My Little Girl*. She knew that getting a part in a Hollywood movie was nearly impossible for an unknown. She believed if she could charm the casting director, however, the part would be hers. Jennifer went into the audition with confidence and, sure enough, she won the role of Myra. In *My Little Girl*, Jennifer played an inner-city teen who is mentored by a rich girl, played by Mary Stuart Masterson. Although it was not a musical, making the movie was still very exciting for Jennifer. Her role was small, but it was exhilarating to see herself on-screen. While dancing and singing were her first loves, she began to consider a career in acting. Since she had already landed a role, she began to think that she could actually succeed in Hollywood. Jennifer knew that her dance career could lead to other opportunities, so she continued her lessons.

Growing Up

Jennifer attended dance classes all through high school. She also studied classical theater. She experimented with singing, dancing, and acting, and she loved all three. Jennifer dreamed of being a performer, but her parents felt it was not a sensible decision. The self-proclaimed daddy's girl wanted to make her parents happy. After graduating high school in 1988, Jennifer enrolled in Baruch College and worked part-time at a law firm. Fueled by her parents' encouragement, Jennifer chose to study law at college. To her family, becoming a lawyer was the ultimate accomplishment. Taking on her father's work ethic, Jennifer worked hard to excel in school. Her classes and job at the law firm kept her extremely busy, but Jennifer continued her dance classes anyway.

Dancing was not just a hobby for Jennifer, it was her passion, and she was extremely talented at it. Against her parents' wishes, she traveled to Manhattan on the subway for auditions and dancing jobs. David and Guadalupe worried about Jennifer, since she worked such late nights. They also worried about the types of people she was around, since she often earned money by dancing at parties. However, Jennifer never drank, smoked,

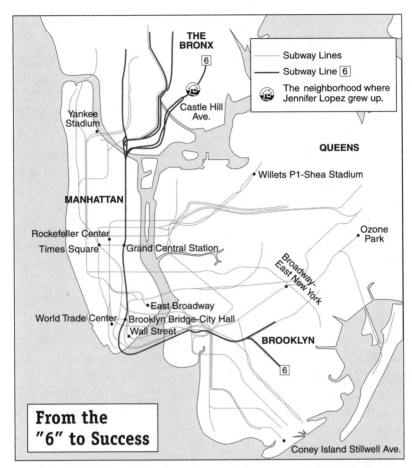

or did drugs, a philosophy she continues to this day. Jennifer went to the parties to dance, and she did not care about anything else. After a semester of school, Jennifer knew she had to pursue her dream full time. Saddening her parents, Jennifer dropped out of college. However, it broke her parents' hearts even more to make the decision that brought Jennifer closer to her dream.

Leaving Home

As soon as Jennifer left college, her parents gave her an ultimatum. She would either reenroll in school or move out of the house. Following her heart, Jennifer left home in a heated argument with her parents. It was extremely hard for her to say good-bye to the house she had grown up in. Even though her parents, in essence, kicked her out of the house, Jennifer remained just as close with them. They hated to see her leave, but they were even more afraid for her. David and Guadalupe believed in Jennifer's talent, but they knew how difficult it was to make it in the entertainment business. They worried that Jennifer would end up broke and living on the street, or that she would get involved in a shady business deal. Besides, they wanted Jennifer to get a college education, no matter what career path she chose. In her neighborhood, going to college was a dream in itself, so when Jennifer proclaimed that she wanted to be a star, she was nearly laughed out of her neighborhood.

Jennifer won a scholarship to a dance school in Manhattan. She moved to an apartment above the school's studio. She spent every day dancing and auditioning. In the late '80s, hip-hop music finally crossed over to the Top 40 charts and Jennifer was excited. Not only did she love to dance to hip-hop since she first heard "Rappers Delight," but she was very good at it. Because she was one of the few dancers who excelled at this style of dancing, she landed several jobs dancing in small-time rap videos. Not one to forget her Latin heritage, Lopez also took part in a Spanish dance company, Ballet Hispanico, where she danced flamenco, ballet, and jazz. Jennifer excelled at all of these forms of dance.

For a year and a half after leaving school, success eluded Jennifer. She still waited for the big break that would lead her to stardom and happiness. Becoming a success was especially important to Jennifer because she wanted to make her sister Leslie proud. Leslie had dreamed of becoming an opera singer in her youth, but after several unsuccessful auditions, Leslie gave up on her dream and became a schoolteacher, just singing in the comfort of her own home.

On the Road

After a succession of one-time gigs, Jennifer landed a long-term job in Europe touring for five months with the show *Golden Musicals of Broadway*. She was excited and scared to go overseas. Soon her excitement turned to sadness when she realized she

Jennifer wanted to achieve stardom, in part, to make her sister Leslie (left) proud.

was the only performer in the show without a solo. Jennifer was heartbroken and turned to the one person she knew could make her feel better: her mother. But Guadalupe did not offer her the sympathy she looked for. "I called up my mom crying because I didn't think I'd been given a fair shake," Jennifer said. "I thought she'd offer me some sympathy. Instead, she said, 'Don't you ever call me crying again! You wanted to be in this business, so you better toughen up!' And I did. That was the best advice I'd ever gotten in my life."[4]

After what seemed like the longest five months of her life, Jennifer returned home to New York from Europe. She immediately began auditioning again. She learned that Fox television was auditioning dancers for a new comedy variety show, *In Living Color.* To Jennifer, being on TV was a sign of success. She went into the audition with steely confidence and wowed the judges. She was a finalist for a dancer position, but she was devastated to learn that she did not win the spot. Temporarily stunned, Jennifer quickly regained her resolve to succeed and she went on more auditions. Dealing with attacks of self-doubt, Jennifer often gave herself a pep talk. "There were times when I was like, 'What am I doing?' I'm not one of these prodigy people. I'm just this person from this small neighborhood in the Bronx, and what makes me think that I'll be able to do movies or sing?" Jennifer said. "But you've got to believe in yourself, because not a lot of people will."[5] Remembering her mother's advice, and believing in herself, Jennifer refused to give up on her dream.

Soon, she landed a spot on a tour of the musical show *Synchronicity.* She traveled to Japan with the musical show, where she served as a singer, a dancer, and a choreographer. She made a conscious decision to enjoy this trip more than her European trip. Although she was busy with the show, Jennifer felt glamorous traveling the world. She knew that several people from her hometown would have loved to do what she was doing. When she got home from Japan, she did not have long to brag about her trip overseas. Soon she learned some exciting, life-changing news. Her dancing career was about to be kicked into high gear.

Chapter 2

In Pursuit of Acting

W HEN JENNIFER LOPEZ LEARNED of the audition for the Fox variety television series *In Living Color*, she believed it would be her big break. Lopez was heartbroken not to make the final cut, but she did not give up. Upon returning from her tour in Japan she got a phone call from Keenen Ivory Wayans, the producer and star of *In Living Color*. A Fly Girl dancer had quit the show and they offered Lopez her spot. She finally was given the chance to make her Hollywood dreams come true.

Finally a Fly Girl

In 1991, the twenty-one-year-old Lopez won the much coveted spot of a Fly Girl on *In Living Color*. However, taking the job meant that she would have to move across the country, to Los Angeles, where the series was filmed. Lopez was not thrilled about the move. She was an East Coast girl at heart and the thought of moving so far away was unpleasant. She knew this was her big chance, though, so she hesitantly packed up and moved to Los Angeles.

Upon arriving in Los Angeles, Lopez found an apartment and began her new career in television. Her new job was exciting at first, but she was still homesick. Unhappy, she spent much of her time on the telephone with her family and long-term boyfriend, David Cruz. Cruz eventually moved to Los Angeles to be with Lopez. Having her love around, Lopez cheered up a bit.

Her time on the show was not as pleasant as she had hoped. Lopez had struck up a close friendship with Keenen Wayans, but

Keenen Ivory Wayans and Damon Wayans perform a skit on In Living Color. *Lopez's first television role was as a dancer on the show.*

some of the other Fly Girls were jealous of their bond. They felt like Lopez was his favorite, and they let her know it. Lopez often received a cold shoulder from most of the dancers. She also felt pressure from her choreographer, Rosie Perez. Perez was extra hard on Lopez, and Lopez felt like the treatment was unfair. But Perez had high hopes for her fellow Latina, so she pushed Lopez to be the best. As time went on, the two became closer friends.

Keenen Wayans's Advice

Early in her career as a Fly Girl, Lopez approached Wayans for acting advice. He already had a successful career as a movie actor, and he had several connections in the movie business. Being in Hollywood, Lopez could not help but get caught up in the glamour of the entertainment business. She yearned to do more than dance in front of the camera; she wanted to act, too. "I'd say to Keenen, 'I want to be an actress! I want an agent!'" Jennifer said. "And he'd say, 'You'll get your chance.'"[6] Lopez was eager to start acting, but Wayans advised her to stick with the show for two years, to save money, and then think about auditioning for other roles. She heeded his advice, and it paid off after exactly two years.

Although she was disliked by several jealous Fly Girls, Lopez made a valuable friendship with one of her fellow dancers. Her new friend happened to be married to a television producer—Ralph Farquhar. He had created a new sitcom, *South Central*, for the Fox network, and he was looking for acting talent. He had also happened to notice Lopez's camera presence on *In Living Color*. Thanks to his wife, Lopez met with *South Central*'s producer, and she auditioned for a role on the series.

Rosie Perez

During her days on *In Living Color*, Jennifer Lopez frequently clashed with the show's choreographer, Rosie Perez. Like Lopez, Perez started out as a dancer and made her way into films. Born Rosa Maria Perez on September 6, 1964, in Brooklyn, New York, Perez dreamed of becoming a star. A talented dancer, she got her start as a dancer on the music show *Soul Train*. She also had a knack for choreography, and she choreographed several music videos. In 1989, she made her film debut in the Spike Lee drama *Do the Right Thing*. Her acclaimed performance led to roles in other films, including *White Men Can't Jump*. In 1993, she gained critical acclaim for her role as a grieving mother in *Fearless*. The performance won her an Academy Award nomination. Perhaps best known for her nasally, heavily Brooklyn-accented voice, Perez is an actress directors go to when they need a spicy, feisty character. In 2000, Perez was arrested for disorderly conduct at a rally to protest military testing on the Puerto Rican island of Vieques. Saucy on-screen and off, Perez continues to act in memorable roles in film and television.

Her Big Decision

Before she learned if she had won the role, Lopez was made an offer most dancers could not refuse. After Lopez had appeared in the Janet Jackson dance video "That's the Way Love Goes," Jackson offered her a spot as one of her dancers for her 1993 summer tour. It was a dream job, especially since Jackson was the biggest pop star at the time. Lopez said yes and began rehearsals. However, before she played even one concert with Jackson, she discovered she had been offered the role on *South Central.* Now Lopez had a decision to make: take the spot on the Jackson tour and solidify her status as a successful dancer or drop out and take her chances as an actress. Since acting had been her dream, she quit the tour and accepted the *South Central* role. Her intuition had finally paid off; her dance career had

Janet Jackson offered Lopez a job as a dancer on her 1993 tour. Lopez rejected the offer for a television role.

paved the way for an acting career. There was no looking back for Lopez. "For a dancer, [the Janet Jackson tour] was one of the best gigs you could get," Lopez later remarked. "I just happened to have other plans."[7]

A Comedic Start

In fall 1993, Lopez said good-bye to *In Living Color* and began her role as wisecracking Lucille, a grocery store cashier, on *South Central*. Lopez loved being on set, memorizing lines, and acting, instead of just dancing, for the camera. Her parents were proud of her, too. In 1993, she also won a role in the television movie *Nurses on the Line: The Crash of Flight 7*, where she played the heroic nurse Rosie Romero. Lopez believed her acting goal was right in front of her. Being on television was one step closer to being a film star. Her giddiness was short-lived, however, as *South Central* was canceled after only one season. Lucky for her, television executives at CBS had noticed her charisma. Lopez stole nearly every scene in *South Central*, and CBS believed she was the perfect fit for a new series they were developing.

In early 1994, Lopez accepted the role of Melinda Lopez in the CBS drama *Second Chances*. Drama was a new challenge for Lopez who excelled at her comedic character on *South Central*. She expanded the emotions she had displayed in *Nurses on the Line: The Crash of Flight 7* and acted in dramatic scenes every week on *Second Chances*. Lopez discovered that she had a knack for both comedic and dramatic acting, and she quickly became the most popular character on the series. However, as had happened with her first series, *Second Chances* lasted only one season. But since Lopez's character was so well liked, CBS created a spin-off show using her character from *Second Chances*. In fall 1994, Lopez starred in *Hotel Malibu*, which centered on her character, Melinda, and her relationship with her family, including her strict father.

Lopez seemed to have bad luck at television, as *Hotel Malibu* became her third consecutive series to fail and go off the air after one season. Still, CBS executives were convinced of Lopez's potential and they offered her a long-term development deal,

Lopez (second from right) poses with the cast of Hotel Malibu. *The CBS show failed and went off the air after only one season.*

which meant they would find a proper and successful series for her to star in. This was a great opportunity for Lopez, since CBS was the highest-rated network at the time, and they had essentially promised she would become a famous television star.

Risking It All

Lopez had the offer of a lifetime in front of her, but intuition told her she was destined for something more. She turned down the lucrative CBS offer to pursue a career in film. Her television experience gave her the confidence she needed to audition for film after film. Lopez was determined to have a career in movies. However, her first few months of auditioning after leaving television were hard. She worried about money and began to doubt that she was made for Hollywood. Several times she contemplated packing up and returning home to New York. But Lopez decided that she would not give up, and she stayed on the West Coast, looking for her next big break.

As she attended parties to make connections and interest casting agents, Lopez discovered the seedy side of Hollywood. "There's a lot of drugs around and everybody drinks. And I never got into that stuff," Lopez said. "[My mother] really instilled in us that that stuff was just evil. I must have had a guardian angel and God watching over me."[8] Lopez refused to get involved in the dark side of show business. She had a goal in sight, and she would not let anything get in her way.

Dream Come True

In 1995, Lopez went on a very important audition for director Gregory Nava. He was casting his new small-budget movie, *Mi Familia*, which was about a Mexican family's history over several decades. Lopez went into the audition to try out for the role of Maria, a young mother. Nava was impressed by her talent, emotion, and confidence and offered Lopez the role. She enthusiastically accepted.

Lopez was thrilled to begin work on *Mi Familia*, especially because it was an inspiring story about Latinos. Maria is a young Mexican girl in the 1920s who works as a nanny after immigrating to Los Angeles. She meets a man named José and falls in love. After marrying and having two children, Maria, pregnant with her third child, is deported back to Mexico. The dramatic story line finds her fighting her way back to her husband and family in California.

For Lopez, her time on the set was not a breeze because she acted in such demanding scenes. Her most memorable scene found her character Maria fighting her way through a raging river across the U.S./Mexico border. Lopez performed the scene herself, without a stunt double. She had to endure a day of shooting in freezing thirty-eight-degree water. She refused to complain or give up. To Lopez, this was the chance to show her

Lopez's river scene in Mi Familia *was one of the film's highlights. Her acting in the drama caught the attention of several directors.*

dedication, and she was not going to lose it. Nava admired her strength and bravery, and the river scene was one of the film's highlights. Although her character was played by another actress in later scenes, as the decades went by, Lopez was one of the film's shining stars. Her ability to hold her own in such a dramatic film caught the eye of several directors. After *Mi Familia*, Lopez found her acting career kicked into high gear, and she began working nonstop.

Money Train

First up for Lopez was a role alongside successful action star Wesley Snipes and television-star-turned-film-actor Woody Harrelson in the big-budget action thriller *Money Train*. Director Joseph Ruben needed a fiery and sassy actress to play the role of Grace Santiago, a love interest pursued by Snipes and Harrelson. In Lopez, Ruben found the perfect star. For Lopez, it was a breakthrough. For the first time, she won a role that was not dependent on her ethnic background. Ruben had not been looking for a Latina actress specifically, and winning the role made Lopez feel like she would not be pigeonholed as only a Latina actress.

Lopez went into the filming of *Money Train* with all of her heart. Her character, Grace, was a tough-as-nails female detective on the transit beat. Snipes and Harrelson played fellow transit cops. Lopez threw herself into preparing for the role. She spent time with real transit cops to see what their job entailed, and she spoke with several female police officers about how they were treated by their male counterparts.

Little did she know that she would be dealing with male ego offscreen, too. Although she was still dating Cruz, Lopez became the object of affection for Wesley Snipes. Both Snipes and Harrelson flirted with Lopez, but she felt like Snipes took it too far. He constantly asked her for dates and even tried to kiss her. Lopez tried to let him down easily, but Snipes took it personally. With a bruised ego, he gave Lopez the cold shoulder throughout the rest of their time on the film set. Lopez, ever the professional, just did her best and ignored Snipes's attitude.

Lopez had high hopes for *Money Train*. It was her first big-budget movie, and she knew that it could make her a star. Audiences, however, were not intrigued, and the film was a box-office bomb. Both Snipes and Harrelson found themselves ridiculed in the press for making such an unsuccessful movie. Lopez's career, however, came out unscathed. Critics noticed her spark and star quality. Although critics thought the film was terrible, they thought Lopez shined. Lopez had no time to think about the film's failure, as she was already on another set.

Learning from Mom

Another director who had noticed Lopez in *Mi Familia* was acclaimed director Francis Ford Coppola, the man behind the
award-winning *The Godfather* films. His next film was *Jack*, a film
starring Robin Williams. Williams plays a boy who ages four
times faster than his real age; as a ten-year-old boy, he had the
body of a forty-year-old man. Coppola needed to fill the role of
a sympathetic, sweet schoolteacher for the film. Coppola was
impressed with Lopez's *Mi Familia* performance and he invited
her to audition for the role of Miss Marquez in *Jack*.

Lopez, who fought back her nerves meeting such a legendary director, went into the audition with her trademark confidence. In reading the script, Lopez displayed the compassion
necessary for the role of Miss Marquez. Coppola offered her the

*Lopez and Robin
Williams perform in
a scene from* Jack.
*Initially, Lopez was
nervous at the
prospect of working
for the film's famed
director, Francis
Ford Coppola.*

role. She had beat out other actresses such as Lauren Holly and Ashley Judd. In 1995, she went to work on the set of *Jack*. As she had done with *Money Train*, Lopez sought out advice for her role as a schoolteacher. However, all she had to do was pick up the phone and call her mother, who was still a schoolteacher. She made a conscious effort to model her character after her mother.

Her time on the *Jack* set was her most rewarding so far. Coppola, who filmed the movie on and near his estate in Napa Valley, California, made the cast and crew feel like family. Lopez was surprised that Coppola was not intimidating. She even compared him to a teddy bear. Lopez also enjoyed bonding with costar Robin Williams. Williams, known for his comedic persona both on-screen and offscreen, kept Lopez laughing with impersonations of other actors. He and Lopez once acted out Romeo and Juliet, with Williams impersonating actor Sylvestor Stallone and Lopez impersonating Rosie Perez's signature nasally voice.

Lopez's boyfriend, Cruz, also played a role in *Jack*. In one of the movie's final scenes, he had a nonspeaking role as the husband of Lopez's character. A real-life marriage between Lopez and Cruz, however, would never happen. Shortly after filming *Jack*, in March 1996, the couple split after ten years together. "At least we're on film together," Lopez said. "We'll always have *Jack*."[9]

The split was difficult for Lopez, but she believed it was necessary for her career. Lopez believed that Cruz, who had yet to make a career for himself in Los Angeles, was holding her back. She needed to be free if she was to make it in Hollywood. After the split, Cruz moved back to New York to open a dry-cleaning business. "Career-wise, we weren't in the same place. He just didn't know what he wanted to do," Lopez said. "But I was so fast. I was like a rocket, he was like a rock."[10]

Jack opened in theaters to moderate success. It was a rewarding role for Lopez. She believed the experience she gained working with a legendary director like Coppola and a high-profile actor such as Williams would further her career. Again, critics praised Lopez's work. It took a charismatic actress to hold her own with such an energetic actor like Williams. She was on her way to being the star she had always dreamed of being.

The Other Jack

Lopez continued to go from set to set in 1996. She auditioned for a role in director Bob Rafelson's film noir *Blood and Wine*. Williams had been a high-profile costar, but the star of *Blood and Wine* was Academy Award–winning actor Jack Nicholson. Nicholson was one of Hollywood's most legendary actors, and several young actors found him intimidating. Lopez, however, was not fazed. She went into the audition and gave it all she had. Rafelson knew he found his star when he met Lopez. Lopez wanted the role because she felt the acting style required for a film noir would be a challenge. She wanted to play as many varied characters as she could, so she would be thought of as a versatile actress.

Lopez flew to Miami to film *Blood and Wine*. In the movie, she plays Gabriella, an immigrant Cuban woman who is the mistress of Nicholson's rich married character, Alex. However, she falls in love with his son, Jason, played by Stephen Dorff. Gabriella stays with Alex because his wealth can help her family back in Cuba, and Jason, who is not wealthy, cannot provide financial support. Gabriella works as the nanny of one of Alex's wineshop customers. The film takes a dramatic turn when Alex schemes to steal a diamond necklace from the same customer with the help of Gabriella. At the end of the film, Gabriella realizes what she missed by staying with Alex, but she knows that she must live with the fate of her decision. Lopez believed Gabriella was a great character that exemplified some of the difficult challenges of being a Cuban refugee.

Her time on the set with Nicholson was well spent. Although Nicholson, who was famous for flirting with his costars, got playful with Lopez, she had a good sense of humor about it. She enjoyed the first scene she filmed with Nicholson, which was a salsa dancing scene. Lopez, the trained dancer, was absolutely at ease. She even taught Nicholson a few steps, and he showed her some swing dancing moves. "I'm happy to report, he only stepped on my toes once,"[11] Lopez said.

Lopez stars with Jack Nicholson in the film Blood and Wine. *Lopez thought her work in the film noir would show directors that she could take on a variety of roles.*

A New Love

During her time in Miami, Lopez fell in love with the city and vowed to make it one of her future homes. She also fell in love with a Miami resident. She and friends frequented singer Gloria Estefan's Miami restaurant, Lario's, during the filming of *Blood and Wine.* Lopez had noticed a cute waiter, and she eventually introduced herself. The waiter, Cuban refugee and aspiring model Ojani Noa, was taken with Lopez. Sparks flew immediately, and they began an intense relationship. Friends and family worried that Lopez, who had just ended the long-term relationship with Cruz, might have jumped prematurely into a relationship with Noa. Awash with love, however, Lopez and Noa became inseparable.

The Big Blockbuster

Immediately after filming *Blood and Wine*, Lopez was at work
again. For her next on-screen opportunity, Lopez was given the
choice between two films: *Fools Rush In* and *Anaconda. Fools Rush
In* was a romantic comedy about an upper-class American man
and a working-class Mexican American woman. *Anaconda* was
an action thriller about a giant snake that terrorized a documentary film crew in the Amazon. Lopez was unimpressed with the
Fools Rush In script and she had tired of playing Latina characters. She took a chance by starring in the gory *Anaconda.*
Mexican actress Salma Hayek eventually won the lead role in
Fools Rush In, which only enjoyed moderate success.

Anaconda was Lopez's first special effects movie. Once again,
her role as documentary film director Terri Flores was not race
specific. Lopez was thrilled to be cast because of her talent and
not her heritage. Lopez flew to Brazil to film *Anaconda.* She enjoyed the hot, tropical weather, but she missed the conveniences
of life in the city. She and costar, rapper turned actor Ice Cube,
were eager to return to Los Angeles to film the second part of
the film. However, her other costars, Eric Stoltz and Jon Voight,
relished their time in the jungle. Ice Cube and Lopez bonded on
the set because of their homesickness and because Lopez was
such a fan of his music. Not one to complain about filming con-
ditions when she was given an opportunity, Lopez gave her all
to her role in *Anaconda.*

Anaconda was not her most dramatically challenging role, but
Lopez loved the finished product nonetheless. She got to play a
tough character who survives the danger, and she knew it would
be the kind of movie that audiences would love. *Anaconda* was
considered a popcorn movie, which meant it was the kind of
film where viewers did not have to think about the plot, they
could just have fun.

With both *Blood and Wine* and *Anaconda* wrapped, Lopez had
worked nonstop. Both films were set to come out in 1997, along
with the next film she would star in—*Selena.* It was the first film
in which she would be the main character—the star—and it
would change her life forever.

Chapter 3

The Breakthrough

BY 1996, TWENTY-SIX-YEAR-OLD LOPEZ had enjoyed moderate success with roles in films such as *Mi Familia, Money Train,* and *Jack.* However, she had yearned for the role that would take her over the top. She wanted to be a movie star, and in 1997 she got her chance. *Mi Familia* director Gregory Nava was casting his new film, a biopic of slain Tejano singer Selena Quintanilla Perez. It was a high-profile film, especially among the Latino community. Selena was a beloved star who had been murdered by the crazed ex-president of her fan club, Yolanda Saldivar, just a year before the film got under way. Nava was under pressure to make the film an accurate and moving dedication to Selena's life. He knew none of this was possible without the right star. Portraying Selena became the role of Lopez's dreams.

The Story of Selena

Lopez could relate to Selena. She, too, was a Latina from a loving but strict family who dreamed of becoming a superstar. Selena, a Mexican American, had risen to fame in the Latino community through her Spanish-language Tejano songs. After forming a Tejano band with her family as a child, Selena quickly became a role model as a bilingual crossover artist. When the twenty-three-year-old former child singer was murdered on March 31, 1995, she was in the process of recording her first English-language album. Selena's death was mourned by her vast fan base who idolized her.

Selena's death was so tragic that, unbeknownst to her father, Abraham, Fox was already developing a film of her life story. Upon reading about the project in the *New York Times,* Abraham

Selena poses with her Grammy in 1994. The immensely popular singer was murdered in 1995, and her story was developed into a movie.

chose to work with Nava on a biopic, in order to ensure that one of the two films would accurately portray Selena's life. Abraham was accused of exploiting his daughter's death, but he had not planned on making a Selena film until reading about the Fox project. Because he was under such scrutiny, he took extra care in relating Selena's story. The movie was also his way to deal with the loss of his daughter.

Becoming Selena

Even though Lopez had already worked with Nava, she still had to audition for *Selena*. She was not alone. More than twenty-two thousand hopefuls auditioned for the part. Lopez's screen test took all day, and it was difficult. She had actually auditioned for *Selena* before leaving to film *Anaconda*, but because the audition process would take time due to the high number of tryouts, she did not find out how well she did until she was in Brazil. When Lopez's agent phoned her to tell her she had won the part, she was so happy that she screamed. Finally, a leading role in a major Hollywood film was hers.

Lopez felt a great amount of pressure with the role of Selena. She wanted to honor the slain singer and she wanted to solidify her status as an actress. She knew this role was a once-in-a-lifetime chance that she may never have again. Lopez was intent on making this her best film yet. Like she had in other films,

The Life of Selena

In 1996, Jennifer Lopez won the role that would make her a star. The film, a biopic of Tejano singer Selena, was a heartbreaking story of fame gone wrong. Lopez campaigned to win the role and she immersed herself into the life of Selena. Her role as Selena is what inspired Lopez to pursue her dream of singing.

Selena Quintanilla Perez was born on April 16, 1971, in Lake Jackson, Texas, to Mexican American parents. Selena showed a musical talent at a young age, and her father encouraged her dream of becoming a singer. He formed a band, comprised of her family members, to play shows around their home state of Texas. She recorded her first album with her family group, Selena y Los Dinos, at twelve years old. Selena sang in Spanish, even though English was her first language. At age sixteen, she won Performer of the Year at the Tejano Music Awards. Only a teen, Selena had a bright future. She signed a deal with EMI Latin in 1989, and released her major label debut the next year. In 1992, at just twenty-one years old and against her father's wishes, she married boyfriend and new bandmate Chris Perez. However, her father forgave her and welcomed Chris into the family. In 1993, Selena won a Grammy Award and began a successful clothing line. After gaining major success in the Latin music world, Selena was in the process of recording her first English album in 1995. However, on March 31, at just twenty-three years old, she was shot and killed by her ex–fan club president Yolanda Saldivar. Selena was gone, but her spirit lived on. In 1997, the film of her life was released. Fans worldwide discovered the music of Selena, thanks to Lopez's inspiring portrayal. After the film was released, two of Selena's English songs, "I Could Fall in Love" and "Dreaming of You," were released to mainstream radio and became instant successes.

Lopez threw herself into researching her character. She watched hours of videotape of Selena in concert and in home movies. She also spent time with Selena's family in San Antonio, Texas, where the movie was filmed. The family let Lopez look at Selena's makeup box, which remained untouched. The box still contained Selena's fake eyelashes and powder puff. Selena's belongings still even had her scent. Having contact with some of Selena's most intimate objects, Lopez felt a strong connection with the singer.

For the performance scenes, the film hired a choreographer to teach Lopez how to dance like Selena. Selena was not a dancer like Lopez; she was never choreographed. Selena got into the music and danced with it. After a few weeks of lessons, Lopez asked the choreographer to stop teaching her because she realized she would never learn how to dance just like Selena. "Selena wasn't a dancer, she was just a natural performer,"[12] Lopez said.

Selena's family spent several days on the set of the movie, which added pressure for Lopez. After her scenes onstage, she would look to Selena's family for their reaction. She felt relieved when Selena's family gave her encouragement. The experience was also emotional for Selena's family. Seeing Lopez onstage, dressed as Selena and lip-synching to her songs, it was like seeing Selena alive again. On many days tears were shed by Selena's family on set. They also embraced Lopez as a daughter figure. "Selena's mother was really wonderful to me," Lopez said. "She was always worried. She'd say, 'You look tired, you're not eating. You're just like Selena, you don't want to eat so you're not fat onstage.' She was very nurturing and caring."[13]

Pleasing the Fans

Although Lopez had the approval of Selena's family, she was not as openly accepted by Selena's fans. The casting of a Puerto Rican in the role of a Mexican American created controversy among the Latino community, according to the media. Lopez did not necessarily look like Selena, which the Mexican American press focused on. Although a prosthetic

Lopez worked hard to accurately portray Selena. The actress watched hours of videotape of Selena and spent time with the Tejano singer's family.

nose was made for the film, Nava chose to film without it. With makeup and a dark wig, Lopez was transformed into Selena. Lopez declared the controversy of a Puerto Rican in a Mexican American role was all hype. Several Selena fans found their way to the set and cheered. When Lopez filmed the opening scene of the movie, a stadium concert with thirty-three thousand cheering fans, she felt support from everyone present.

While Selena was a role model to the Latina community, Lopez became a groundbreaker with her role as Selena. She was the first Latina since 1940s actress Rita Hayworth to have a starring role in a film. But that was not all. Lopez received $1 million for the film, the highest amount ever paid to a Latina actress. It was more money than Lopez had imagined, but with it came even more pressure. With this milestone, she believed she had to make the film a success. The attention she received also added stress. The success of the film was riding on her. She had to prove that she could carry a film. If she failed in such a high-profile role, she feared she may never be given a chance like it again. She tried to ignore the pressure and do a good job. She felt honored to be in her position. "I felt a lot of pressure," Lopez said. "People were saying, 'Oh, she's making this much money and she's the first to do this.' You think to yourself, 'How do I follow up with that? How do I keep that going?' Then I realized . . . how lucky I am."[14]

The Thrill of Performing

Although Lopez did not sing in *Selena*, she did lip-synch to Selena's voice. Being onstage, in front of Selena's fans, Lopez felt what it must have been like for Selena. Dancing for thousands of screaming fans, and getting caught up in the music, Lopez was reminded of performing in musicals in her younger days. She had always enjoyed singing around her house, with the stereo and in the shower, and she thought she had a decent voice and could make it in the music industry. Toward the end of filming *Selena*, she began to seriously think about pursuing a singing career. It was another lofty goal, but she had proven herself by going from a dancer to an actress. Although she was busy, she vowed to pursue music in the near future.

After four months of filming, work on *Selena* came to an end in late 1996. Lopez had felt an emotional connection with Selena throughout filming, but it was not until she saw a rough cut of the finished film that the reality of Selena's death hit home. While watching the movie, Lopez broke down into sobs. She was overcome with sadness at Selena's loss. Even though she had never met Selena, she felt like she had become a friend or a sister because she had come to know her so well.

Head over Heels

Selena's life story also made Lopez realize that life was short. When Selena was murdered, she was a newlywed. Selena had married her guitarist, Chris Perez, against her parents' wishes. When Chris joined Selena's family's band, there was an undeniable attraction. The couple kept their relationship a secret from Selena's father, because he had wished she would focus on herself and her career. He thought love would just get in the way. Unwilling to deny her love, Selena eloped with Chris. After an initial shock, the family welcomed him into the family.

Lopez could relate to Selena's passion about her love life. When Lopez fell in love, she fell head over heels. Her new boyfriend, Ojani Noa, flew to Texas to be with Lopez during the filming of *Selena*, even though her parents disapproved of their new relationship. David and Guadalupe Lopez were traditional and they would have preferred that Lopez be married instead of living with her boyfriend. They would soon get their wish.

Selena's wrap party was a huge bash. It was the last time that Lopez would see several of the Texas-based crew members. It was also a celebration of Selena's life and the labor of love her movie had become. Lopez enjoyed dancing on the dance floor with Noa throughout the night. However, during one dance, Noa dropped to his knees and proposed marriage to Lopez, retrieving a diamond ring from his pocket. Although partygoers advised her to think about her decision, she answered an enthusiastic and tearful yes. The couple had only been dating for a few months.

Lopez could not wait to tell her friends and family of her engagement. But instead of encouragement, they told her to take it slow. She had not known Noa for long, and how was she to be sure that he was the one? Noa did not have an established career. He had been content so far to follow Lopez to film sets. However, those closest to her worried that he was not good enough for her. They feared the couple might have a rocky relationship as Noa dealt with Lopez's rising fame. She did not want to listen to naysayers. After all, she was in love, and she followed Selena's example. After a whirlwind engagement, the couple married in Miami on February 22, 1997, in front of two hundred friends and family. Lopez and Noa enjoyed a relaxing honeymoon in Key West, Florida. After working nonstop for more than two years, Lopez took a much deserved break. She and Noa had a great time spending their days on the beach and enjoying the weather. It was very romantic to be with her new husband in such a tropical locale. As a married couple, they chose to split their time between Miami and Los Angeles.

Becoming a Star

Lopez had filmed her last three films in a row, and they were all set to be released in a span of two months. On February 28,

Against the advice of friends and family, Lopez married Ojani Noa. The couple had only known each other for a few months.

1997, *Blood and Wine* opened to minimal success. It was disappointing for Lopez, but she did not have to worry for long. On March 21, 1997, *Selena* premiered. Suddenly, Lopez was everywhere. *Selena* took in more than $50 million at the box office. Her performance in the movie made viewers take notice. Critics lauded her performance, and she became a star overnight.

Lopez had dreamed of becoming a star, but the instant success was overwhelming. She could not walk down the street without being recognized. She fully realized what fame meant one day in Miami. Incognito, she went outside to exercise and ended up drawing attention. "I was jogging by myself," Lopez said. "I had on my glasses and my heart monitor and my hair was in a ponytail—my mother wouldn't even have recognized me. But all of a sudden, I hear people shouting 'Lopez! Lopez!' I'm thinking, 'Surely, they can't be talking about me.'"[15]

On April 11, 1997, *Anaconda* opened. It was not a critical favorite, but fans seemed intrigued. Thanks to word of mouth and the appearance of new star Lopez, the film earned more than $100 million in the United States alone. Men mostly enjoyed the film because of the special effects and action. Women mostly wanted to see the film because of Lopez. *Anaconda* only cost $30 million to make, a low figure for a special effects movie. The profits made it a blockbuster. Lopez, who had always believed in the film, was happy that it was a success.

Nineteen ninety-seven was the best year of Lopez's life. She could not believe how quickly her dreams were coming true. She was especially happy to make her parents proud. Lopez used part of her *Selena* paycheck to buy a brand new Cadillac for her mother. When she led her blindfolded mother to the car, which was wrapped in a red ribbon, her mother could barely hold back her excitement. And when Lopez saw the look on her mother's face, she was so proud. It was a bittersweet return to her neighborhood and the neighbors who never thought she would make it.

Jennifer the Perfectionist

Nineteen ninety-seven was also the busiest year of Lopez's life. She had literally worked nonstop and the stress was beginning to get to her. Her body was telling her to slow down, but her perfectionist nature took over. Although most actresses would have been content with a starring role in a film such as *Selena*, Lopez still wanted more. She had already come this far, but she knew she was meant to be an even bigger star. She was stressed, tired, and almost to the point of a mental breakdown, but she refused to take time off.

Lopez dove right into her next project in the midst of 1997. She won the role of Grace McKenna in the Oliver Stone film *U Turn*. In the film, Grace is a Native American, small-town Arizona woman married to the powerful Jake, played by Nick Nolte. After Bobby, played by Sean Penn, is stranded in her town, he becomes transfixed by Grace. Grace is a manipulative character who yearns to get out of her town. After Jake meets Bobby, he offers him money to kill Grace. Grace then offers Bobby money to kill Jake. All three characters become embroiled in a twisted and dramatic story line.

Second Chances

Filming *U Turn* was not Lopez's first time meeting Oliver Stone. Years earlier, when she was a struggling television actress, she read for a role in the film *Noriega*, which was about political dictator Manuel Noriega. As Lopez read the script, Stone spent the audition cleaning his office. Lopez was offended and incensed. She stormed out of his office, cursing, and vowed to never work with him again. Plans for *Noriega* were eventually scrapped. Meanwhile, Lopez was on her way to superstardom. It was sweet revenge for the scorned actress.

When Stone called to ask Lopez to audition for the role of Grace in *U Turn*, she bitterly declined. She then decided to give him another chance. With her $1 million role in *Selena*, she felt like she had the upper hand. She was also touched that he called her personally and wished to make amends. She chose to meet with him to read the script and see if it was worth her time. She was not expecting it, but she found that Stone was quite likeable. She had a great time talking to him. Lopez showed Stone her true personality: tough and self-assured. The famed director was so charmed that within minutes of Lopez leaving his office, he called her agent to say the part was hers.

Lopez had changed her mind about Stone, but then a situation arose that made her lose her trust in him again. After actress Sharon Stone showed interest in the role of Grace, he met with her. He knew Lopez was Grace, but he felt pressure from his studio head to meet with Sharon Stone. Lopez began to feel like she should not work with him. Maybe her first instincts were right. In the end, Sharon Stone realized she was wrong for the character and bowed out of the running. The role was Lopez's. The first day of filming, Oliver Stone took Lopez aside and apologized for the situation. He told her she was always his first choice. Stone and Lopez became friends during the shoot and learned to laugh off their rocky past.

Lopez also enjoyed working with Sean Penn and Nick Nolte. Although both had reputations for being intense, she showed no

Lopez and Sean Penn act together in a scene from U Turn. *Lopez initially turned down the role of Grace in the Oliver Stone film.*

In 1998 Lopez received an American Latino Media Award (ALMA) for her role as Selena. She also won ALMA's Lasting Image Award.

fear. Both respected her confidence, and they sensed that she was not intimidated to be on set with them. Many actresses fell victim to their intimidation and became shy. Not Lopez. She even admitted that she felt a bit of an attraction to Penn. However, because both actors were married at the time, it stopped at an innocent flirtation. Lopez's appearance in *U Turn* made her a critical darling. She was praised for holding her own with such commanding actors. Her last string of critical and commercial successes foretold an exciting and rewarding film career for Lopez.

Being Honored

As if her rising stardom was not enough of a gift, the end of 1997 and the beginning of 1998 were especially rewarding to Lopez. First, *People* magazine named her one of the 50 Most Beautiful People of the Year, an honor only given to A-list stars and those on the cusp. In 1998, Lopez won an American Latino Media Award (ALMA) for her role in *Selena*. She also won ALMA's Lasting Image Award. The state of Texas awarded her the Lone Star Film & Television Award for Best Actress for *Selena*. She was even more shocked to learn that she was nominated for a Golden Globe Award for the same role. She felt like a glamorous princess dressing up in a beautiful designer gown for the Golden Globes. Although she did not take home the award, she went home feeling like a winner. She was on her way to Hollywood's A-list, and she was beaming with pride.

It would not be until her next role that Lopez would go from rising star to superstar. In a newspaper interview for *Selena,* she predicted what would happen next. "I think if I did really well in one role, in just one great role, that would put me over the top,"[16] she said.

Chapter 4

On Top of the World

In 1998, Lopez was one of Hollywood's brightest new stars. A successful starring role in *Selena* had solidified her status as a newcomer to watch. She had worked hard to achieve her goal of becoming a movie actress, and she insisted on pushing herself more. She had already won more success than most in her hometown would have thought possible. Now that she was showing that she would succeed in everything she predicted, it was time to make a bigger move, so she could become an even bigger star.

Out of Sight

In 1998, Lopez auditioned for the role of Karen Sisco in director Steven Soderbergh's film *Out of Sight*. Karen was a tough female detective, who, against her better judgment, falls in love with escaped convict Jack Foley, played by George Clooney. The script was savvy, witty, and engaging, and Lopez knew it was the role for her. However, as she had encountered with *U Turn*, a more successful actress showed interest and she had to wait to audition. Universal Pictures, the studio that made *Out of Sight*, wanted Sandra Bullock to star. Bullock was a proven fan favorite, and she could bring moviegoers to theaters. But when Soderbergh and Clooney met with Bullock, they asked her to screen test. Bullock, who was at the level where she did not have to audition, refused. Lopez, who wanted the role, was more than happy to screen test. In Lopez they hoped to find the perfect saucy personality to counter Clooney's smooth and suave character. Even their screen test was oozing with chemistry. Clooney and Lopez re-created one of the film's opening scenes. In the film, the couple are locked in a car trunk, but for the screen test they did the scene on a couch. Soderbergh set a camera in a spot in the room to make it look as though they were scrunched up in a trunk. In reading her flirty but tough lines, Lopez wowed Soderbergh. He had captured on film the kind of chemistry he was looking for. Even Lopez knew the role was hers before leaving the audition. She impressed both men and won the role.

Although the heritage of her character had not been determined, Italian actor Dennis Farina portrayed her father, so it was assumed that she was Italian. However, Lopez pointed out that Karen's mother, who had passed away, was not pictured in the film, so she could have easily been Latin. The role, however, was not specific to any ethnicity. Lopez was honored that Soderbergh recognized her talent and cast her anyway. "He just saw me and he thought I was the best person for the role," Lopez said. "I said I didn't think there should be any jokes about cheeky chica or anything referring to the fact that

Lopez stars with George Clooney in Out of Sight. *Director Steven Soderbergh cast Lopez after a screen test proved that she and Clooney work well together.*

I'm Latin. That's not important for this movie. He said, 'I absolutely agree.'"[17]

Lopez received $2 million for her role in *Out of Sight*, although she asked for $5 million. Since it was a fairly small-budget film, $5 million was out of the question, but Lopez felt empowered to request it. Although she did not get the figure she had hoped for, Lopez gave 100 percent of herself to the filming of the movie. This role was important to Lopez. She realized it would take her over the top. The movie was just as important to Clooney. A successful television actor, Clooney longed to make the crossover to film. He had already starred in the box-office flops *One Fine Day*, with Michelle Pfeiffer, and *The Peacemaker*, with Nicole Kidman. His previous costars became real-life friends, but on-screen they lacked the chemistry needed to make a film magic. Clooney and Soderbergh both saw in Lopez a spark. She was a superstar in the making, and this film would show that to the world. On set, Clooney was an endless source of support to Lopez and the rest of the cast. Both actors took a different approach during filming. While Lopez focused intently on building her character, Clooney goofed off between takes. He played jokes on the cast and crew and enjoyed daily basketball games. Lopez, the perfectionist, and Clooney, the player, were opposites offscreen, but on-screen they sizzled.

Honest Interview

Prior to the release of *Out of Sight*, Lopez gave an interview to the American film magazine *Movieline*. Talking to writer Stephen Rebello from a poolside chair, she spoke her mind on costars,

The Making of *Antz*

In 1998, after working back-to-back on movie sets, Jennifer Lopez provided her voice to the animated feature *Antz*. Lopez starred as Azteca, a worker ant. She worked with acclaimed filmmaker Woody Allen on *Antz*. She enjoyed trying a new type of film, as it offered an entirely new kind of challenge. "It's very different from acting on film," she said in an interview with CBS's Mark McEwan on September 30, 1998. "You know, you're in a room with a microphone by yourself. There's no other actors there. And basically, they just give you your lines to read, so it takes a lot of imagination."

In a 1998 interview, Lopez made negative comments about actresses Cameron Diaz (left) and Gwyneth Paltrow (right). Lopez later claimed she was misquoted.

fellow actresses, and many other topics. She spoke openly about the advances Wesley Snipes made on the set of *Money Train,* and she spoke of Nicholson's flirting on the set of *Blood and Wine.* But when Rebello asked her thoughts on several of the up-and-coming actresses at the time, she made comments she would regret. About Cameron Diaz, Lopez said, "A lucky model who's been given a lot of opportunities I just wish she would have done more with."[18]

When asked about actress Gwyneth Paltrow, Lopez dismissively said, "Tell me what she's been in. I swear to God, I don't remember anything she's been in."[19] She was most scathing in her comment about Madonna. "Do I think she's a great performer? Yeah. Do I think she's a great actress? No. Acting is what I do, so I'm harder on people when they say, 'Oh, I can do that. I can act.' I'm like, 'Hey, don't spit on my craft.'"[20] She also dismissed actresses such as Winona Ryder and Claire Danes. Lopez came out sounding arrogant and catty. For *Movieline*, it was the ultimate celebrity interview, but for Lopez, it was potentially fatal to her career.

Immediately after the issue of *Movieline* hit newsstands, media outlets picked up on the interview. Snippets were quoted in numerous articles, and soon it was known all over Hollywood that Lopez had badmouthed several actresses. Upon reading the finished article, Lopez felt like she had been misquoted. She insisted that her comments were taken out of context and that she did not mean what she had said. She and her publicist immediately went on damage control, publicly apologizing and sending flowers to the actresses she had mentioned.

Her apologetic actions were too little too late. Lopez was already shunned by the actresses mentioned, and she was branded a self-absorbed diva, a label she would fight hard to lose. Lopez was also branded "difficult" to work with by several Hollywood bigwigs, and she eventually lost her publicist, who quit because of Lopez's negative image. Although the backlash was immediate, it soon was forgotten, although both Paltrow and Madonna continue to have indifferent opinions of Lopez.

The lesson Lopez learned was to be more careful in future interviews. "I learned that you have to be careful how you state things, particularly for a print interview," Lopez said. "It's different from TV, because the audience doesn't see you speaking. They don't see the context. In the end, the thing that bothered me was that somebody might have been hurt by what I said. Also, it gave people a false picture of me. I'm not a catty person."[21]

When the finished result of *Out of Sight* was released, her controversial interview was forgotten. No matter what her attitude, Lopez had finally become a star.

Out of This World

On June 26, 1998, *Out of Sight* was released in theaters and moviegoers loved seeing Clooney and Lopez sizzle. Their chemistry was praised by fans and critics alike. Although the movie was a success for both actors, and Clooney finally proved himself as a leading man, it was Lopez the critics focused on. They called her a revelation and a superstar.

Lopez had praise for the film, too. Not only were the performances great, but, besides *Selena*, it was her favorite film she had done. Lopez felt like she had surpassed the ingenue status and had proven herself a leading lady opposite a powerful male lead. She knew *Out of Sight* would make her a star, but she did not realize the extent her sexy performance would take her.

The Body

In *Out of Sight*, Lopez received full sex-symbol status, primarily because of her curvaceous body. At the time, Hollywood was full of stick-thin actresses such as Gwyneth Paltrow and Calista Flockhart. Lopez, although a slim size six, had a voluptuous body with curves and a pronounced backside. Many female fans who were tired of the impossibly thin look of popular Hollywood actresses approved of the body image that Lopez projected. Of course, many male fans appreciated Lopez's looks as well.

Lopez never once felt she was not thin enough to be a movie star. She adored her curves ever since she was a girl. After all, her love of dancing had shaped her body into the physique she adored. Her husband called her La Guitarra because her body was shaped like a guitar. In fact, she believed her full-figured body was an advantage to her career. "Beauty is in diversity. I never felt weird going to Hollywood knowing I didn't have the same body type as other people," Lopez said. "My body made me different, it made people turn their heads."[22]

Critics and fans began to take serious notice of Lopez's acting abilities with her role in Out of Sight. *Her curvaceous figure also made her a sex symbol.*

Her Biggest Fan

Lopez's appearance in *Out of Sight* garnered the attention of many of Hollywood's elite, but one high-profile fan in particular felt the need to work with her immediately. Rapper and music producer Sean "Puff Daddy" Combs got in touch with Lopez through her manager. He was about to film a music video for his new song "Been Around the World." He had been watching Lopez and her career, and he remembered that she began as a talented dancer. When Lopez returned his phone call, Combs told her he believed it was time to remind the world that she could dance as well as act. She thought it was a good idea and agreed to appear as his love interest in the video. The idea of being on a music video set again was exciting to Lopez, especially since she had been seriously considering a career as a singer.

On set, Lopez wowed Combs with her dancing skills, and the couple showed a spark immediately. Lopez thought Combs was charming, and he fell in love with her personality. There was just one hitch: Lopez was still married. Lopez and Combs became fast friends and enjoyed a purely platonic relationship for months.

Sean Combs

In 1999, Jennifer Lopez went public about her relationship with rapper Sean "Puff Daddy" Combs. Some fans were shocked that the glamorous actress would date a rapper, but the couple had striking similarities. Combs, a Harlem, New York, native, began his career as a dancer, and also started his own clothing line, Sean John. Combs and Lopez shared a drive to succeed.

Combs was born on November 4, 1969. He got his nickname "Puffy" in high school because of the way he could puff out his chest to make his body look bigger. He was ambitious ever since he was a child, when he made thousands of dollars a month just as a paperboy. As a teen, he began dancing in music videos. During one shoot, he noticed that the people behind the scenes, or the producers, were the real moneymakers in music. He decided to pursue a career in music production. While a student at Howard University, he began interning at Uptown Records. Making the grueling four-hour commute from Washington, D.C., to New York was taxing on the young man, but he saw his future in his grasp. He eventually dropped out of school and took a full-time job at Uptown, becoming the youngest Uptown employee. He produced multiplatinum debut albums for Mary J. Blige and Jodeci. In 1993, he left Uptown and began his own label, Bad Boy Entertainment. He produced stars such as Faith Evans and rapper Notorious B.I.G., his best friend. After B.I.G. was killed in a 1997 shooting, Combs pursued his dream of becoming a rapper. He wrote and recorded the No. 1 song "I'll Be Missing You," which was a tribute to his fallen friend. Combs's debut album, *No Way Out*, went platinum and was the beginning of a successful career. After meeting Lopez in his 1998 music video for "Been Around the World," the couple started dating after a long friendship. The pair dated for almost three years until Lopez broke it off in 2001. Since the breakup, Combs has continued to be both a successful rapper and producer, overseeing albums for artists such as Dream and B2K.

When Lopez married Ojani Noa, it was against the wishes of those who knew Lopez better. Just as they had expected, the marriage began unraveling within a year of the wedding day. Lopez denied the marriage problems in the press, and she tried to make it work. However, as she felt with Cruz, Noa had a hard time dealing with Lopez's new male fan base and her rising stardom. He was proud of her success, but he wished she could be more of a traditional wife who spent more time at home. When Lopez could not bring him on location, he missed her terribly. Part of him wished he could be the moneymaker of the family. Lopez had worked too hard to let that happen. She chose to let the relationship go before being asked to choose love over success. In June 1998, the couple divorced, after only sixteen months of marriage.

With Noa out of the way, Lopez could finally give in to her growing attraction to Combs. In Combs she found a kindred soul. Like Lopez, Combs was always a dreamer. Growing up in Harlem, New York, he had lofty goals. At a young age, he listened to rap music and dreamed of being a rapper himself. Also like Lopez, he had started out as a dancer, performing in several music videos before crossing over to producing. As a teen, he became the youngest executive at Uptown Records, producing such breakout acts as Mary J. Blige and Jodeci before forming his own label, Bad Boy Entertainment. For the first time, Lopez had found a partner who would not be intimidated by her success. Lopez also enjoyed the attention Combs paid. He lavished her with gifts and provided endless compliments. Combs made Lopez feel like a beautiful princess.

Musical Support

Not only did Combs provide Lopez with romantic inspiration, but he also encouraged her to pursue her dreams of recording an album. After recording the soundtrack to *Selena* in 1997, Lopez had been working on recording a demo CD of Spanish songs, which she financed with her own money. Her manager, Benny Medina, had been sending the discs to various record companies, but the right deal had not come along yet. In 1998, the perfect opportunity presented itself.

Unbeknownst to Lopez, Sony Music president Tommy Mottola had seen *Selena* and phoned a friend to predict that Lopez could become a music star. When he learned that Lopez desired a record contract, he immediately asked to meet with her. Lopez traveled to New York and met with Mottola in his posh office. Nerves were not an issue when Lopez met Mottola. She knew he was giving her a chance to record for one of the most powerful record labels in the world, and she was not about

Lopez and Sean Combs met when he asked her to dance in his music video. The relationship turned romantic after Lopez divorced Noa.

*Sony Music president Tommy Mottola predicted that Lopez would become
a music star. He offered Lopez her first record contract in 1998.*

to miss it. When Mottola asked Lopez what she really wanted,
she patiently and confidently told him that she wanted to make
a great album. Mottola did not need any more explanation,
since he was intent on signing her that day. Before she accepted
the deal, Mottola called in all of the producers who would work
on her debut album. Among the producers who met with Lopez
one by one were R&B producer Cory Rooney, who would executive produce the effort. She also met with producer-artist
Babyface and acclaimed hip-hop and soul producer Rodney
Jerkins. By bringing in successful producers, Mottola hoped to
woo Lopez into accepting the Sony deal. "Tommy laid out the

red carpet," Rooney said. "He was letting her know that if she took the deal, basically we'd make you a star."[23]

At the end of her day of meetings at Sony, she joined Rooney and Mottola in Mottola's conference room. Rooney played Lopez a song he had worked on, which she would have the chance to sing on her album. Lopez loved the song and told him so. Mottola immediately told her to go to the recording studio the next day, even though the deal was not even done. Lopez, both excited and slightly overwhelmed, agreed, and work began on her debut album the very next day.

In the Studio

Lopez was a pro on a movie set, but in the recording studio, it was a different story. She had recorded her demo in a small studio, but Sony's studios were big and elaborate. Walking into the studio, Lopez felt exhilarated. She could not wait to see her album in stores, even though she had months of recording to do. On her first day of recording, when she stepped into the soundproof booth to sing, her producers tried to make her comfortable. They asked if she would like to turn the lights off or burn some candles. Lopez asked why, and they told her that was what other successful singers did in the studio to set the mood. Upon

The Marketing of Lopez the Singer

In 1999, as the release date of Jennifer Lopez's debut album neared, Sony Music president Tommy Mottola went to work on promotion. In the months before the album's summer release, Mottola began Lopez's marketing campaign. He organized street teams to generate buzz about Lopez, with flyers all over New York City, and especially her native Bronx. Soon, posters featuring Lopez's not-yet-released album were in schools, restaurants, and bars, and her music was sent to Spanish-language radio stations.

Sony targeted music fans just like Lopez, who enjoyed both urban hip-hop music and traditional Latin salsa music. "My music is a kind of hybrid, the music somebody like me would like," Lopez told Sarah Gristwood of the *Guardian* in a 1998 article titled "Mouth of the Border." "Someone who grew up in the Bronx, of Latin descent but a very American family. I have a lot of street smarts because of the neighborhood I grew up in." Mottola's work paid off when Lopez's album, *On the 6*, debuted at No. 1.

hearing that, Lopez decided that if everyone else did it, she would do it, too.

When it came to her songs, Lopez wanted control. Although few artists actually have control over their debut albums, Lopez succeeded in working with her executive producer, Cory Rooney, on her songs. Mottola and Sony had the majority of the control, but they allowed Lopez to write lyrics. Lopez had never written a song before, but being in the studio and hearing the music, she was inspired. One day Rooney told her to try to write her own song. He worked with Lopez on one song, in which the music was written but the lyrics were not. She felt insecure. She wanted to write a great song, but she did not know how to go about it. She had an idea, but how would she put it into words? That night at home she thought about it and took her ideas to Rooney the next day. Together they wrote her song "Should Have Never." Lopez felt extremely proud to have a songwriting credit on her album. She believed that having a song come from her heart would help listeners relate. With that personal attachment to her albums, the songs truly became her own.

Celebrating Her Latin Heritage

For her debut album, Lopez was already working with the best R&B and hip-hop producers in the music business. But it was also important that she record Latin-flavored songs as well. She turned to the most famous Latin producer at the time, Emilio Estefan. Emilio Estefan, the husband and producer of successful Latin superstar Gloria Estefan, was charmed by Lopez at their first meeting. He offered to help her on her debut album, and she was pleased. Gloria Estefan was an idol to the Latin community, and Lopez knew that Emilio Estefan was the driving force behind his wife's career. Gloria Estefan, who had just finished an album of her own, had a song that she had written but did not have room for on the album. The song, "Let's Get Loud," was a party song with a Latin beat. Lopez fell in love with the song the minute she heard it. Emilio told Lopez that Gloria had asked him to see if Lopez wanted to use the song. "I was like, 'Omigod, yeah! Give it to me! Please give it to me!'"[24]

Lopez enlisted the help of Latin producer Emilio Estefan for her debut album. Estefan's wife, singer Gloria Estefan, allowed Lopez to use one of her songs on the album.

With a song from Latin music's most famous diva on her album, she asked friend Marc Anthony, a famous salsa singer, to collaborate on "No Me Ames," a Spanish love song. Anthony had asked Lopez to appear in one of his music videos and she said yes with one catch—he had to sing on her album. They struck a deal. Lopez appeared in Anthony's video, and Anthony went into the studio with Lopez. Lopez adored the finished product and praised Anthony. Immediately tabloids began to link them as a couple. Lopez, however, was still dating Combs, even though she continued to publicly deny it. She and Anthony laughed off the rumors, which would haunt them for months.

A Little Extra Help

Before finishing her album, Lopez turned to her boyfriend, Combs, for help. Although he had encouraged and supported Lopez in her album, he had tried to stay out of the studio. She was in good hands with the producers Sony provided, and he did not want to get in the way. But both Lopez and Sony realized that a collaboration with Combs could be golden. Combs had a Midas touch when it came to producing, which meant nearly everything he was involved with went gold or platinum. He also had the street credential that Lopez needed to have a mainstream album. With Lopez's Latin appeal and Combs's hip-hop presence, her debut album had the potential to be a huge crossover hit.

By early 1999, Lopez's debut album was finished. Now she needed a title. She had originally planned to title the album *Gypsy*, but she felt it was not right. Finally the perfect title came to her. She decided to name the album *On the 6*, after the number six subway train she rode from the Bronx to Manhattan to take her to auditions when she was just starting out. "My dreams were all born riding on that train," Lopez said. "It couldn't be a more perfect title."[25]

Now all Lopez had to do was wait. She was happy, but also a little scared. If this album failed, she would be a joke—just another actor who wanted to be a singer. Other actors such as Bruce Willis and Eddie Murphy had recorded albums in the past, but the albums were flops. Lopez crossed her fingers and hoped she would be an exception. Her musical career was riding on this album. If she planned on pursuing a long-term musical career, *On the 6* had to be a success.

Chapter 5

A Star Is Born...Again

Luckily for Lopez, she did not have long to wait to find out how her debut album would fare. In early summer 1999, Lopez released her first single, the Rodney Jerkins–produced "If You Had My Love." It became an instant radio hit, soaring to the No. 1 spot on the Billboard singles chart. The music video was an MTV hit as well. In the video, Lopez showed off her dancing skills and wore skimpy outfits to show off her beautiful body.

On the 6 was released June 1, 1999. Due to the strength of her single "If You Had My Love," and curiosity from her film fans, *On the 6* debuted at No. 1 on the Billboard albums chart. She knocked fellow Latin singer Ricky Martin out of the top spot, and her album wound up selling more than 8 million copies worldwide. Lopez, as a musician, had arrived.

The Diva

Lopez spent the next several months enjoying her status as a musician. She loved to make videos, and fans loved to watch. She enjoyed the attention she got from her new fan base. People who had never even seen any of her films shouted her name on the street. Lopez was finally at the level of superstardom she dreamed about. Even though she made an effort to be friendly with every fan she met, the media had labeled her a diva. Lopez's affinity for the finer things in life and her love of shopping had given her a bad reputation. Other critics argued that her constant striving to be number one was a sign of an uncontrolled ego. The image was hard to lose, and she would continue to carry the diva label throughout her career.

Lopez's first album, On the 6, *was a smash hit. It sold more than 8 million copies worldwide.*

Coming Clean

In the months following her album release, interviewers constantly asked her to admit that she was dating Sean Combs. She had thanked someone she referred to as her "Superstar" in her album notes, and journalists assumed it was Combs. Not even Oprah Winfrey succeeded in persuading Lopez to talk about her relationship on her television show interview. On September 9, 1999, the truth came out. The couple attended the MTV Video Music Awards hand in hand. Although it was already widely speculated that they were a couple, Lopez and Combs succeeded in surprising fans at the awards ceremony.

Now that the year-long relationship was out in the open, Lopez felt free to talk about Combs. However, the romance came under media scrutiny. Even fans could not understand what a glamorous woman like Lopez saw in a tough rapper like Combs. She admitted the couple had their differences. Combs liked to go to parties and nightclubs. He would regularly spend thousands of dollars on champagne alone. Lopez, who did not drink, liked to spend her evenings at home. "I'd much rather go to work and come home at night," she said. "My life is quieter. We balance each other out. He gets me out and we enjoy ourselves. Sometimes I make him stay home."[26]

The Arrest

With Combs in her life, Lopez found herself out on the town more often. Several times she convinced him to stay home for romantic nights. However, one night when she begged him to stay home, their night out turned tragic. Excited about the upcoming new year, Combs brought Lopez and a few friends to Club New York in Manhattan on December 27, 1999. The couple had a great time dancing and wishing clubgoers a happy new year. Toward the end of the night, things got out of hand. Combs, known for enjoying his wealth and status, had gone around the club, giving people high fives. When Combs went over to high-five another male partier, the man refused to cooperate. This was offensive to Combs, and the men got into a heated argument. Then the man threw a handful of money at Combs, mocking his wealth and claiming that he, too, had money. At that point, the argument turned physical and the club atmosphere turned chaotic. Jamal "Shyne" Barrow, Combs's protégé, came to his defense. Barrow was carrying a gun and fired a few shots into the air. Bystanders Natania Reuben, Robert Thompson, and Julius Jones were all struck by stray bullets.

Confused and afraid, Combs grabbed Lopez and Barrow and fled to their waiting car. The car sped off and ran eleven red lights before being stopped by police. The car was searched and the gun was found. Everyone in the group, including Lopez, was arrested. Shaking with a mix of fear and anger, Lopez was hand-cuffed and taken to the police station. Lopez clearly had nothing to do with the shooting, but she was still held at the station for fourteen hours.

A victim of being in the wrong place at the wrong time, Lopez was upset and worried about Combs. If he would have been willing to stay home that night as she had hoped, they

This mug shot was taken at the police station after Lopez was arrested. She was released without charges after being held for fourteen hours.

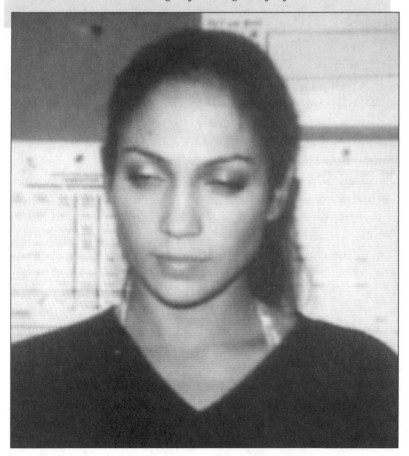

would not have been in the tragic situation. Lopez sat in the main area of the station, and because of the buzz their arrest had generated, there was a high number of officers there. Lopez felt like they were all staring at her as if she was a caged animal in a zoo. When one sympathetic officer asked if he could get her anything, she requested a bottle of cuticle cream, which he ran to the store to get. Lopez tried her best to remain calm, even though she worried about what her parents would think. "I had never been arrested before and I don't plan to ever be again. I tried to stay calm because I knew I hadn't done anything,"[27] she said.

For Lopez, the worst part of her arrest was facing her parents, who were scared after hearing of the shooting on television. The morning after the arrest, David Lopez had turned on his television and heard that his daughter was involved in a nightclub shooting. He had no idea whether or not his daughter was alive. David and Guadalupe thought the worst. Luckily, Lopez asked Medina, her manager and friend, to phone her parents. Medina assured them that their daughter was safe, and they were relieved. However, they began to fear for Lopez's future with Combs, whom they felt was responsible for the arrest.

Backlash

Lopez's parents were not the only ones to question her safety with Combs. Medina, who had previously been Combs's manager, advised her to leave the relationship, as did the rest of her professional team. Her management and representation feared that her relationship could cause her to lose her broad audience. They feared for her future in film and music. Even the press weighed in. "The New York tabloids had three or four pages at a time just on whether Puff and I should break up," Lopez said. "I don't wish an experience like this on my worst enemy."[28]

Although Lopez was released without charges, Combs was not as lucky. He was charged with weapons possession and bribery, after his driver alleged Combs had offered him money to take responsibility for the gun. Combs, a millionaire, paid his bail and was set free until his trial, which would not happen for more than a year. Lopez and Combs tried to continue a normal relationship after the arrest. Although everyone around her advised her to rethink the relationship, she and Combs remained inseparable.

Going to the Grammys

In February 2000, Lopez and Combs attended the Grammy Awards together. It was less than two months after their high-profile arrest, and they hoped to leave their past behind them. Lopez was nominated for Best Dance Recording for "Let's Get Loud." She had become a designer's darling, and she had the choice of several gowns to wear. Although they were all gorgeous and expensive, only one dress could be the winner. Designer Donatella Versace had designed a green, barely-there dress, which had an open back and front. The dress was held on only by double-sided tape.

Combs proudly brought Lopez down the red carpet in her headline-grabbing dress. Amid gasps and camera flashes, her dress became the biggest story of the night. Then, when she took the stage with actor David Duchovny to present an award, the world saw her dress. The crowd reaction told Lopez that her dress was the perfect choice. At first the crowd was silent and shocked, then suddenly they erupted into loud applause and screaming. Duchovny commented that for the first time in his

The Dress

In 2000, Jennifer Lopez was nominated for her first Grammy Award. But it was not the nomination that people wanted to talk about, it was her scandalous Donatella Versace dress. Lopez remembered the magical moment she tried on her dress prior to the awards ceremony. "My stylist collected stuff for me to look at," Lopez told Michael Fleming of *Playboy* in September 2000. "She knows what I like. I loved that dress. I'd seen it on Donatella Versace, who wore it to the Met one night. Two days before the Grammys, it came my way. The first time I tried it on, I felt the impact when I walked out of the bathroom. My make-up artist, my manager and Puff were looking at me. Puff was like, 'That's the one!' The reaction shows that you can't ever plan how people will react."

Actor David Duchovny and Lopez present an award at the 2000 Grammys. Lopez's revealing dress made headlines for weeks after the event.

life, he was sure that no one was looking at him. Lopez ended up losing her Grammy Award to Cher, but her dress made headlines for weeks.

The Cell

In summer 2000, after taking a two-year break from films, Lopez starred in the psychological thriller *The Cell*. She had read the dark and edgy script five years earlier and loved it. Lopez was not a big star when she first had read the script, so movie studios were afraid to take such a risk casting an unknown in such a high-budget film. By 2000, she had the choice of movies, and she wished to rekindle interest in *The Cell*. In a meeting with Mike De Luca, head of New Line Cinema, she convinced him to make the film.

Lopez plays Catherine Deane, a therapist who enters the mind of a comatose serial killer to discover the location of his lair, where his last victim is trapped in a cell that is filling with water. Eclectic music video director Tarsem Singh, who goes by his first name, made *The Cell* his first feature film. Known for his cinematography skills, Tarsem's *The Cell* was full of lavish colors and eye-catching effects.

To prepare for her challenging role, Lopez read books about dream interpretation and spoke with a therapist. In the film, Lopez wore several elaborate costumes and often looked unlike

As a big star, Lopez was able to convince New Line Cinema to produce The Cell. *She prepared for her challenging role by researching dream interpretation.*

herself. She was proud of the finished result, and likened it to *Silence of the Lambs* in its macabre and suspenseful effect. No doubt propelled by her successful music career, *The Cell* was a box-office hit. It brought in more than $60 million. *The Cell's* success was sweet for Lopez because she was a certifiable triple threat—actor, singer, and dancer. Even her one-time idol, Madonna, had yet to find the film success Lopez had achieved. Lopez believed that anything was possible, and she looked forward to a long career of doing exactly what she wanted to do. "I want everything," Lopez said. "I want to do good work. I think of people like Cher and Bette Midler and Diana Ross and Barbra Streisand. That's always been the kind of career I'd hoped to have."[29]

The Birth of J.Lo

Lopez spent the end of 2000 working on her sophomore album. Once again, Rooney and Combs were on hand for support. Lopez hoped to outdo her debut. With this album, she was confident and in control of her writing. It was a far cry from her debut, when Rooney had to convince her to try writing lyrics. This time, Lopez was executive producer and had final say on every song included. She hoped to make this album more personal than her last by writing four songs on the album.

Combs also contributed a song, "That's Not Me," about a relationship gone wrong. Lopez said the song was about the moment in a relationship when one has had enough and must get out. In interviews, reporters asked if the song was a comment on Lopez's relationship with Combs. She denied it was autobiographical and vowed that her relationship was rock solid. Critics could not help but compare her first single, "Love Don't Cost a Thing," to Combs and Lopez. In the song, Lopez sang from the point of view of a woman whose mate showers her with gifts and money but not enough attention. It was widely known that Combs lavished Lopez with clothes, jewelry, and even a car. She denied that this song, too, was about Combs.

When it was time to name the album, she wanted to choose a title that meant something. Loyal fans had given her the nickname J.Lo, and she liked it. She chose to honor her fans by titling her album *J.Lo*. The nickname took over, though, and from then on, Lopez was referred to as J.Lo. At first she thought it was cute, but after a few months, it became annoying. Now Lopez was a one-named artist like Cher or Madonna, much to her chagrin. She knew it had gone too far when her mother once called her J.Lo.

The Wedding Planner

While recording her new album, Lopez worked a second job on the set of *The Wedding Planner*. She starred as Mary Fiore, a wedding planner who falls in love with the fiancé of a powerful client. For Lopez, the film was important because it was her first comedic lead. The film started off with a bit of a controversy when actor Brendan Fraser, who had signed on to star opposite Lopez, dropped out of the film. Tabloids were quick to link tension between the stars to his resignation, but Fraser dropped out of the film to star in another film, *Bedazzled*. He thought he would be a better fit for *Bedazzled*.

Lopez was not without a leading man for long. Texan Matthew McConaughey took over the role. She and McConaughey had convincing chemistry and the shoot went smoothly. "I believe that God has a plan for everything," Lopez said. "I think it was supposed to be Matthew all along."[30]

Lopez received $9 million for her role in *The Wedding Planner*. It was her biggest paycheck yet. Her character, Mary, was an Italian woman with a loving father and workaholic lifestyle. Lopez felt a connection with her character. She could relate to her need to constantly work, even though her love life suffered. Mary put her heart on the back burner as she strived to be at the top of her game. Similarities were eerie, especially because during the movie's filming, Lopez's relationship with Combs was unraveling.

Change of Heart

While filming the video for "Love Don't Cost a Thing," Lopez became close to a dancer named Cris Judd. Judd and Lopez had briefly met months earlier, but sparks flew on the video set. Judd was sympathetic and understanding, and he comforted Lopez over her failing relationship. Their friendship quickly turned to love, and the couple began secretly dating. Lopez had essentially broken up with Combs, but denied it in the press to protect him as his trial began in January 2001. She even appeared to be a devoted girlfriend as she attended his trial dates and testified on his behalf.

Combs was reluctant to let Lopez go. To try to win back her love, he had one hundred white doves and one hundred pink balloons released into the air outside her home. Two weeks later, he asked friend and legendary soul singer Luther Vandross to serenade her. Nothing worked. The relationship was all wrong for Lopez, who needed to focus on her career if she wanted to achieve the next level of stardom.

J.Lo was released on January 23, 2001, and went straight to No. 1. *The Wedding Planner* hit theaters January 26, and also went to No. 1. Lopez became the first person in history to have both the top album and the top film simultaneously. She sold an impressive 272,252 copies of *J.Lo* in the first week. She was thrilled about her accomplishment, especially because the milestone had nothing to do with being a Latina. Lopez did not have time to celebrate, though, because she was on a promotional tour for her album and film.

Meeting Ja Rule

For her second single from *J.Lo*, Lopez released the album version of "I'm Real." It was one of Lopez's favorites from the album, but radio reception was lukewarm, and it did not get much airplay. Sony decided the song needed something extra. Rapper Ja Rule was called in to meet with Lopez. He had written a hip-hop remix of the song for a duet and she liked it. Radio disc jockeys immediately put the remix into heavy rotation, and the video became a hit as well. Her third single, "Ain't It Funny," got the remix treatment, too, thanks to Ja Rule. Both songs became No. 1 hits, and Lopez received equal play on both rap and pop radio. Her fan base nearly doubled. Although Lopez praised Ja Rule and seemed thankful, critics accused her of using the rapper for street credential. Her singles were failing on their own. They only became successes with Ja Rule's participation. He was often credited for saving her career. However, the practice of a rapper-singer collaboration became more widespread after "I'm Real." Lopez and Ja Rule are credited for inspiring a new brand of duet.

Lopez and Ja Rule perform together at the MTV Awards. The two are credited with creating the hip-hop duet.

Ja Rule

Jennifer Lopez owed much of her musical success to rapper Ja Rule, who rewrote and guested on two of her biggest hit songs, "I'm Real" and "Ain't It Funny." Born February 29, 1976, in Hollis, Queens, New York, Ja Rule, or Jeffrey Atkins, began rapping as a teen. In 1995, he signed with TVT Records. Only one single was released with the small record label before he signed with a major label, Island/Def Jam. Ja Rule was known for his grizzly voice and tough records when he was paired with Lopez. After the success of their collaborations, Ja Rule found a new mainstream audience. Suddenly, he was more successful than ever before. His next single, "Always on Time," featuring newcomer Ashanti, hit No. 1 in 2002. Due to the strength of his singles, Ja Rule has gone multiplatinum with every release.

The Breakup

After months of denying any trouble in their relationship, Combs issued a statement on February 14, 2001. He was still in the midst of his trial, but he could not deny the breakup any longer. Weeks later, Combs was found innocent of all criminal charges from the nightclub incident, but he had already lost Lopez. Although she preferred to avoid discussion of Combs in interviews, Lopez still insisted the couple, at one time, were very much in love. "Our relationship was so in the press that people didn't really take it as a serious relationship, but we really loved each other," Lopez said. "There was a time we really were two people who fell in love and it didn't work out. I realized that it was something that wasn't right for me."[31]

With the breakup known, Lopez felt free to step out in public with Cris Judd. The couple were quickly becoming serious. Judd supported Lopez, and he was content to stand by her side. Lopez enjoyed the relationship because she had control. For the first time, she was in a relationship with a man who did not mind that she was the moneymaker of the couple. With two successful albums, a hit movie career, and a new love, Lopez felt like her life could not be better.

Chapter 6

Love at Last

By spring 2001, Lopez was one of the biggest stars in music and film. She had achieved dreams she had had since childhood. Lopez was happy with her career, and with new love, Cris Judd, by her side, she felt like she was close to having a lasting love. With her new power in Hollywood, she yearned to branch out in other areas of expression.

Lopez the Designer

Lopez chose to add entrepreneur to her résumé in 2001. In April, she collaborated with Andy Hilfiger, the younger brother of designer Tommy Hilfiger, to create Sweetface Fashions. Their first project was a line of women's clothing called J.Lo. Lopez designed the line that included jeans and velour sweatsuits. The items often featured small Puerto Rican flags on the labels. The line got off to a shaky start, but soon J.Lo velour sweatsuits became one of the year's most popular trends.

To find inspiration for her clothing line, Lopez looked back at her childhood. She remembered how she used to alter her own clothing for a better fit. Designing clothes for J.Lo was an entirely new form of expression for Lopez. It was just as exciting as acting or singing. "Designing for J.Lo gives me the same adrenaline and creative energy that songwriting does,"[32] Lopez said.

Lopez was busy, but she was glad to create the label. However, unlike other designers, she chose not to be involved in the specifics. She contributed design ideas and her name, but the daily operations were something she simply did not have time for. Eventually Lopez hoped to remove the J.Lo tags from the clothing, so the line could have its own identity. She was worried that her public persona would affect the clothing's sales.

Too Much

Nonstop work had taken its toll on Lopez. She was a workaholic by choice, but by spring 2001, Lopez was exhausted, but it was not a normal exhaustion. She felt nervous all the time and had anxiety attacks. She began to feel like she was having an emotional breakdown. She also felt sick, so she scheduled medical tests. After having an EKG and CAT scan come back as normal, she went to a new doctor. She hoped he would diagnose what was truly wrong with her, so she was exasperated after he told her all she needed to do was eat better and get more sleep. Unconvinced, she ignored his advice at first and continued to obsess over her condition. But after she decided to give it a try, it did the trick. More sleep and a healthier diet made Lopez feel as good as new. Within days, she was back to work. The experience made Lopez realize that she had to be good to her body and mind. "Sometimes I think it was just a reminder to realize it's not about work all the time,"[33] Lopez said.

Lopez and Andy Hilfiger answer questions about their new clothing line at a news conference in 2001.

Angel Eyes

Lopez had a busy year planned, so she knew she had to take care of herself. First, she starred in the thriller *Angel Eyes*, as a police officer, a role she was used to by now. In the movie, her character, Sharon, meets a man named Catch, played by Jim Caviezel, after he saves her life. As she falls in love with Catch, he insists he is her guardian angel. His presence helps her deal with childhood demons, and she becomes a happier person. Lopez described the characters as two lost souls who find and heal each other. It was a dramatic turn for Lopez, and it reminded filmgoers of her acting talent.

Second Marriage

In summer 2001, Lopez felt great. Her music career was in high gear, she had a proven track record in film, and she had a great boyfriend. In August 2001, Judd surprised Lopez by proposing. The couple had been dating less than a year, but Lopez accepted. Friends and family were reminded of her first marriage, and advised her to take it slow. Her family adored Judd and gave their blessing anyway. Lopez had glowed since meeting Judd and he seemed to complement her well.

Just one month later, on September 29, Lopez and Judd were married in a secret ceremony in Calabasas, California. She wore a Valentino gown, and her lawyer, Barry Hirsch, officiated the ceremony. The wedding was successfully kept under wraps, but some paparazzi did learn of the event through insider tips. Lopez was stunned at the effort the photographers made to snap a valuable photo of the wedding. "We had three or four people who climbed up the side of the mountain, trying to get a picture. It was crazy,"[34] Lopez said.

The media picked up on the story and ran with it. Even fans could not believe she would marry Judd so soon. To her, however, it made complete sense. The first few months of her marriage were ultimate bliss. He accompanied Lopez everywhere she went, and she had his utmost attention. She even spoke of starting a family with Judd when the couple had time. Of course, she showed no interest in slowing down just yet.

Lopez and Cris Judd married in September 2001. The couple had been dating less than a year before they wed.

Her First Concert

In November 2001, NBC aired Lopez's first concert. "Jennifer Lopez: Live in Concert" was taped in Puerto Rico, her family's homeland. Stepping onstage, she was reminded of filming *Selena*'s big performance scene. She even spoke about Selena onstage and sang her song "I Could Fall in Love." The crowd went wild.

This concert was important on many levels. She wanted to show that she was an energetic performer, and she wanted to prove her singing ability. Ever since the release of her first album, she had been bothered by rumors that alleged her singing was computer enhanced. She believed that by singing live, she could prove the rumors wrong. Lopez enjoyed her concert experience. She loved the rush of adrenaline and the chance to show off her musical skills.

The New Year

Two thousand one was a banner year for Lopez, but she vowed that 2002 would be even better. In February, she kicked off the year with a No. 1 album release. *J to tha L-O* was filled with remixes of songs from *On the 6* and *J.Lo*. The album contained her duets with Ja Rule, dance mixes of songs like "Waiting for Tonight," and her current single, "I'm Gonna Be Alright." For her new single, Lopez collaborated with Nas, who was one of her favorite rappers at the time. Her husband, Judd, appeared in the video, which was filmed in the Bronx. On set, Lopez waved and smiled at fans who gathered to catch a glimpse. She liked the energy of filming back home. The summer-themed video was all about being outside in the Bronx on hot summer days, basking in the sun, and playing baseball with neighborhood kids. Lopez went from her fun video set straight to a more serious role with her next film.

Enough

In spring 2002, Lopez put the finishing touches on her movie *Enough*. The dramatic film showed Lopez like she had never been seen before. In the movie, she portrays Slim, an abused wife who, along with her daughter, must escape her cruel husband, played by Billy Campbell. Lopez focused all of her energy on the film, which she thought was her most empowering work yet. In this film, it is up to Slim to rescue herself.

To prepare for the role, Lopez, as usual, did extensive research. She spoke with abused women at shelters and got into the best shape of her life. In the film, Slim learns Krav Maga, the martial art of the Israeli army. Krav Maga is an intensely physical form of self-defense. Lopez began training two months in advance. She was sore after every workout, but also exhilarated.

She wanted to do her own stunts convincingly, so she knew she had to learn Krav Maga correctly. In the film, Slim uses Krav Maga against her 6'4" husband. Lopez was thankful that the big fight scene was not filmed until late in the shooting, so she could continue training. Lopez received $10 million for her role, and her bruises proved that she really did earn the paycheck.

Enough was both physically and emotionally challenging. Costars at first doubted that Lopez could handle the shoot. Noah Wyle, who has a role in the film, admitted that he had been fooled by her diva reputation. But he was happily proven wrong. "I wondered if I'd be working with the J.Lo entity," Wyle

Lopez did extensive physical training to prepare for her role as Slim in Enough. *Learning Krav Maga, an Israeli martial art, enabled her to perform her own stunts.*

said. "The first day I worked with her was the morning after the Oscars, and I thought, 'She'll be hung-over. She was out late.' But she was there before me, in full make-up and wardrobe."[35]

For the film, Lopez and Judd cowrote the song "Alive." Judd thought of the piano melody in October 2001, one month after the terrorist attacks on the United States on September 11. With the melody in mind, Lopez thought about her *Enough* character and what she had been through. Writing the song made Lopez realize that life was short and that she was happy to be alive. With the song, Lopez and Judd proved they were a great team. Little did they know that their happiness would be short lived.

Gigli

For her next film, Lopez took the role of gun-toting lesbian Ricki in *Gigli*. The action comedy costarred Ben Affleck. Although the pair were opposites—Lopez was serious about her role and Affleck was a joker—they became friends. Both admitted to preconceived notions of each other. Affleck feared she would be a diva, and Lopez worried he would be a smooth-talking jerk.

Ben Affleck

Ben Affleck was born in Berkeley, California, on August 15, 1972. Raised in Boston, Affleck met best friend and fellow aspiring actor Matt Damon during childhood. Affleck wanted to act since he was a child, and at the age of eight, he won a role in the PBS series *The Voyage of the Mimi*. Affleck's teen years were spent acting in television movies. In 1993, he found fame as a bully in the 1970s comedy *Dazed and Confused*. In 1995, he appeared in the Kevin Smith movie *Mallrats*. The director and actor formed a close friendship, and Affleck starred in multiple Smith films, including his star-making turn in 1997's *Chasing Amy*. Also in 1997, Affleck cowrote the film *Good Will Hunting* with Damon. The best friends also starred in the picture, and won a 1998 Academy Award for Best Screenplay. Affleck's career was nonstop after the win. He appeared in blockbuster films such as *Armageddon* and *Pearl Harbor*. In 2001, Affleck checked himself into Promises Rehabilitation Clinic in Malibu, California, for alcohol addiction. After successfully beating his addiction, Affleck starred in the 2003 action film *Daredevil*. In 2003 and 2004, he has a lineup of films to be released, including *Gigli*, his costarring effort with Lopez.

Shortly after meeting they realized they had more in common than they had thought. However, tabloids ran stories that the actors despised each other and butted heads on set. Sick of the rumors, Affleck took out a full-page ad in Hollywood trade papers *Variety* and the *Hollywood Reporter* praising Lopez as an actress and a person. She was touched by his gesture, and their friendship was cemented throughout the filming.

No one on the set could deny that the actors had a chemistry. They enjoyed flirty banter, but since Lopez was married to Judd, she fought back her true feelings for Affleck. Affleck knew Lopez was off-limits but he could not help developing a crush. Affleck made Lopez laugh with his jokes and by reciting popular rap songs at the time. He was also there to show support when she opened a restaurant, Madre's, in Pasadena, California. The restaurant, which serves Puerto Rican and Cuban cuisine, is run by Lopez's ex-husband, Ojani Noa. The couple had remained friends over the years, and she trusted the restaurant in his hands. Although she claimed it was a neighborhood restaurant, it reflected her classy taste. Antique fans adorned the walls and forty chandeliers hung from the ceiling. She hoped to give the restaurant a tropical feel. To celebrate the opening, Lopez held a glitzy party that was attended by stars such as Affleck, Nicole Kidman, and Brooke Shields.

Maid in Manhattan

With *Gigli* wrapped, Lopez flew to New York to film her next project, *Maid in Manhattan.* She stars as Marisa Ventura, a Bronx woman working as a maid in a fancy Manhattan hotel in this retelling of the Cinderella story. In a case of mistaken identity, a Senate hopeful, played by Ralph Fiennes, thinks she is a socialite after catching her trying on a guest's designer suit. Before he gives her the chance to tell him the truth, he whisks her off for a date. Marisa falls in love with him and must eventually reveal her true identity.

Lopez could relate to her character. Marisa aspired to be more than a housekeeper, but her surroundings made her doubt herself. Lopez remembered what it was like when she was a young dreamer in the Bronx and her neighbors tried to make her give up on her hopes. Making the film, Lopez realized that one reason she has worked so hard was because she had to prove her neighbors wrong. "Being from a Latin community, there is this fear of success because of a fear of failure," Lopez said. "Those kind of things hold people down. That mentality exists. I do feel that I always have to be proving myself through one thing or another throughout my career."[36]

Surprising Split

Lopez spent the summer of 2002 in New York filming *Maid in Manhattan*. Unlike previous sets, Judd stayed home in Los Angeles. It was an ominous sign of what was to come. Soon af-

Lopez smiles at the grand opening of her restaurant, Madre's. The restaurant serves Puerto Rican and Cuban cuisine.

ter, Lopez announced her split with Judd. The pair had only been married for eight months. Neither gave a reason for the divorce, other than that it just did not work out. The split was surprising to friends and family because Jennifer seemed head over heels in love with Judd. Lopez claimed it was an amicable split with no third party, but *Gigli* and *Maid in Manhattan* crew members knew better. She had obviously fallen in love with Affleck while filming *Gigli,* and he regularly visited the set of *Maid in Manhattan.*

The pair denied a relationship, but photographic evidence of the couple together proved otherwise. On July 24, 2002, Affleck celebrated Lopez's thirty-second birthday on the *Maid in Manhattan* set. He even surprised her with an expensive Harry Winston diamond bracelet. After blowing out the candles on her cake, Lopez and Affleck disappeared to her trailer for hours. After the story hit newspapers, the pair were officially outed as a couple.

Affleck had previously dated actress Gwyneth Paltrow, who was brainy and serious. Lopez's most well-known relationship was with rapper Combs. They seemed the most unlikely pair, and fans were shocked. To Lopez, it did not matter what anyone thought. Affleck had charmed her, and they were in love. She felt bad for Judd, especially because he was such a nice guy, but being with Affleck just felt right.

This Is Me . . . Then

Affleck inspired her as she made her third album. At night, after filming scenes from *Maid in Manhattan,* Lopez traveled to a recording studio to lay down tracks for her new album. She had more control than ever, and she wrote several songs, including "Dear Ben" and "Glad," about Affleck. He even helped her with the title. She had struggled with what to call this effort and he suggested *This Is Me . . . Then.* He told her it referred to her being able to give the album to her children or grandchildren to let them know what she was like at that time.

Her first single, "Jenny from the Block," inspired controversy when Bronx natives proclaimed that Lopez had sold out. Even though on the song she sang about still being the same

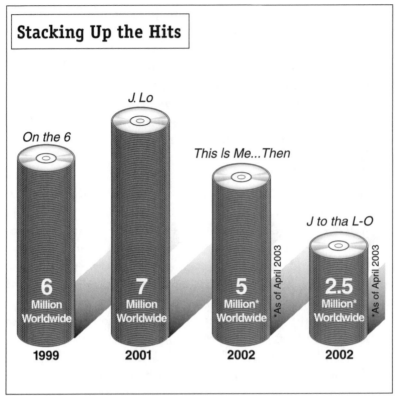

Stacking Up the Hits

J. Lo

On the 6

This Is Me...Then

J to tha L-O

6	7	5	2.5
Million	Million	Million*	Million*
Worldwide	Worldwide	Worldwide	Worldwide
1999	2001	2002	2002

*As of April 2003

*As of April 2003

neighborhood girl, she filmed the video in Los Angeles, a disappointment to fans. Critics and fans alike found it hard to take "Jenny from the Block" seriously. Lopez had completely transformed into a Hollywood starlet, a complete change from the Bronx girl she was when she started out. In the video, Lopez chose to make fun of her star status by depicting her life with paparazzi following her every move. Affleck even appeared in the video as himself. It was his first time on a video set, and he thought it was fun.

Jersey Girl and Glow

Affleck and Lopez so enjoyed working together that they chose to pair up again in the film *Jersey Girl.* In the film, the couple play a married couple that ends in tragedy. Lopez is only in the film for a short amount of time, as her character dies while giving birth to the couple's child. The film centers around Affleck's

Going Home

On December 6, 2002, Jennifer Lopez traveled back to the Bronx to perform at the Kips Bay Boys & Girls Club. Since it was the club where she used to take dance lessons, the homecoming was especially sweet. Current dance students performed a dance routine for Lopez, and she loved it. To the students, Lopez was an inspiration, a girl from their neighborhood who made it big. Lopez's visit was a huge day at the club. Even NBC's *Today Show* filmed the visit. Talking to *Today's* Matt Lauer on December 6, 2002, about the day, she began to get emotional. "This is where it all began," she told Lauer. "This is such an emotional day for me. It's like coming full circle, and just showing how much I do love and appreciate where I came from. It means everything to me that they all came out so early in the morning. I know a lot of people here have a lot of dreams, and I'm living proof that you can do whatever you want to do."

Lopez performs at the Kips Bay Boys & Girls Club in the Bronx in 2002. As a child, she took dance lessons at the club.

character's journey as a single father. Kevin Smith, who directed the couple in *Jersey Girl,* praised their chemistry. Fighting some claims that the Lopez-Affleck love affair was for publicity purposes, he spoke openly of how much they loved each other.

In the midst of a new love affair and busy film career, Lopez launched a fragrance, Glow, with cosmetics giant Coty. Lopez, a perfume addict, took a hands-on approach to choosing the right fragrance. She expressed the smells she liked: soapy, clean, and fresh. After the right combination was found, she named it Glow. The perfume, unlike her clothing line, was an instant success after its August launch. It became one of retail's top-selling perfumes. Lopez was on a roll, both professionally and personally.

The Big Surprise

On November 13, 2002, after weeks of speculation, Lopez told *Primetime Live*'s Diane Sawyer that she and Affleck were engaged. During the televised interview, she told Sawyer the story of the romantic proposal.

The couple visited his hometown of Boston for a weekend with his family. Upon arriving in town, Lopez could tell that

The New Elizabeth Taylor

In 2002, Jennifer Lopez had jumped from one relationship to another before landing with Ben Affleck. Before announcing her engagement to Affleck, Lopez had been married twice and had two long-term relationships. Lopez has not been single since she was fifteen years old, when she met her first love, David Cruz. Her marriage to Affleck would be her third, and she was only thirty-two years old. Lopez's love life garnered a comparison to another great Hollywood diva who could not make her love life work—Elizabeth Taylor. Taylor, the legendary Hollywood actress, was married eight times, twice to the same man. Lopez welcomed the comparisons, as Taylor was a legendary star. "I'm not mad if people call me the modern-day Liz Taylor," Lopez said in an *In Style* article titled "J. Lo on a High," written by James Patrick Herman. "We've all had a love of our life and failed love affairs. I'm just the biggest romantic. It's really sad. I tell people that, but nobody listens. They're too busy writing about the thread count they think I demand."

News of Lopez's engagement to actor Ben Affleck became public in November 2002. The two met while working on the film Gigli.

Affleck felt nervous, but she did not know why. On the way to his childhood home, she tried to find out why he was acting so nervous, but he would not tell her. When the couple arrived at the house, they went to the front door and Lopez saw small candles lining the stairs. Lopez thought his mother had placed them there because she had heard that Lopez liked candles. How sweet, she thought. Then Affleck led her inside the house, which was blanketed with rose petals. Then she noticed that her song "Glad" was playing on the stereo. Lopez was overwhelmed by the gesture and she asked how he was able to set it up. He told her his mom helped, and Lopez started sobbing. She was touched by how his mother had been so inviting. As Lopez cried tears of joy, Affleck pulled out a letter he had written for her and began reading. He proclaimed his love over and over again. At the end of the letter he asked Lopez to marry him, while holding out the engagement ring. The ring, a 6.1 carat, pink diamond, was a rare find, and expensive. Affleck spent $1.1 million on the ring. When Lopez saw the ring was pink, she refused to look at it. As if the proposal was not enough of a romantic gesture, she could not believe he bought her a pink diamond. The experience was so over-

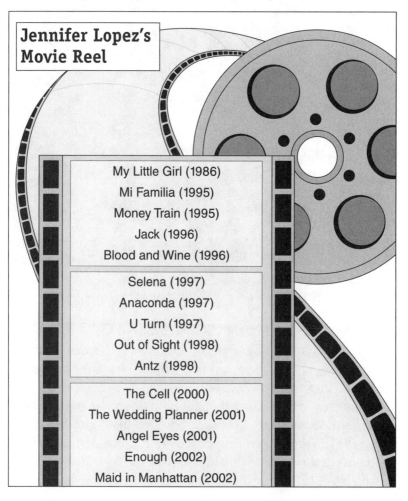

Jennifer Lopez's Movie Reel

My Little Girl (1986)
Mi Familia (1995)
Money Train (1995)
Jack (1996)
Blood and Wine (1996)

Selena (1997)
Anaconda (1997)
U Turn (1997)
Out of Sight (1998)
Antz (1998)

The Cell (2000)
The Wedding Planner (2001)
Angel Eyes (2001)
Enough (2002)
Maid in Manhattan (2002)

whelming that she feared she could not handle looking at the ring. When she finally looked, with Affleck's coaxing, she was amazed and forgot to answer his question. When he reminded her that she had not told him yes or no, she immediately said yes, in between sobs. "I had cried a lot over sadness and relationships that didn't work out," Lopez told Sawyer. "For the first time in my life, I cried an incredible purging of tears of happiness. It was the most cleansing feeling and the most wonderful feeling I ever had. It was the best day of my life."[37]

Overnight, Lopez and Affleck became the couple to watch. Nearly every day another rumor surfaced of their wedding date or location. Lopez has said she is excited about her third trip down the aisle. She likes to say that she has been married twice but has yet to have a marriage. To make their relationship work, Lopez and Affleck worked out a schedule so that they would never work at the same time. They promised that since only one of them would work at a time they could spend quality time together.

The Future

Lopez now hopes to take her acting career to the next level. In 2003, Lopez began work on *An Unfinished Life* with director Lasse Hallstrom. Lopez plays a single mother who must move in with her estranged father-in-law. It is her most dramatic role yet, and movie insiders claim that if she succeeds, she could be nominated for an Academy Award. It is an honor Lopez would love to have. "An Oscar would be fabulous,"[38] she said.

Lopez has a full slate of films for 2003. She is set to star in the crime thriller *Tick Tock* and the romantic drama *Shall We Dance?* For Lopez, her career has always been her top priority. Another marriage may or may not be in her future.

As she nears her mid-thirties, she realizes she needs to grow up. Becoming a mother is beginning to sound more appealing. "I have a wonderful life, it's busy and full," Lopez said. "But my work doesn't complete me as a person. What will complete me is a family. I want to feel the love between a mother and child. Watching your children grow up and have kids of their own. That's going to be more fulfilling than anything I've ever accomplished in my life. I mean, it's just real."[39]

Notes

Chapter 1: Destined for Stardom

1. Quoted in Sarah Gristwood, "Mouth of the Border," *Guardian*, November 20, 1998, p. 4.
2. Quoted in Anthony Bozza, "Jennifer the Conqueror," *Rolling Stone*, February 15, 2001, p. 44.
3. Quoted in Barney Hoskyns, "Jennifer Lopez," *Interview*, April 1997, p. 50.
4. Quoted in Amy Longsdorf, "Blood, Sweat and Tears," *Allentown Morning Call*, February 25, 1997, p. F1.
5. Quoted in Robin Pogrebin, "What Jennifer Lopez Really Wants," *Ladies Home Journal*, January 2003, p. 74.

Chapter 2: In Pursuit of Acting

6. Quoted in Lucy Kaylin, "The Goddess," *GQ*, December 2002, p. 250.
7. Quoted in Kaylin, "The Goddess," p. 250.
8. Jennifer Lopez, interview by Diane Sawyer, "J.Lo," *Primetime Live*, ABC, November 13, 2002.
9. Quoted in Bruce Westbrook, "A Tough Act to Follow," *Sunday*, July 28, 1996, p. 8.
10. Quoted in Stephen Rebello, "The Wow," *Movieline*, February 1998, p. 48.
11. Quoted in Longsdorf, "Blood, Sweat and Tears."

Chapter 3: The Breakthrough

12. Quoted in Kaylin, "The Goddess," p. 250.
13. Quoted in Prairie Miller, "Selena Interview with Jennifer

Lopez," *Ethnic News Search*, July 27, 1998, p. 1.

14. Jennifer Lopez, interview by Mark McEwan, *CBS This Morning*, CBS, September 30, 1998.

15. Quoted in Longsdorf, "Blood, Sweat and Tears."

16. Quoted in "Jennifer Lopez: Take Me As I Am," *San Francisco Examiner*, April 10, 1997, p. E1.

Chapter 4: On Top of the World

17. Quoted in Gristwood, "Mouth of the Border," p. 4.

18. Quoted in Rebello, "The Wow," p. 48.

19. Quoted in Rebello, "The Wow," p. 48.

20. Quoted in Rebello, "The Wow," p. 48.

21. Quoted in Michael Fleming, "Jennifer Lopez," *Playboy*, September 2000, p. 59.

22. Quoted in Fleming, "Jennifer Lopez," p. 59.

23. Quoted in Bozza, "Jennifer the Conquerer," p. 44.

24. Quoted in Chris Connelly, "Jennifer Lopez," May 1, 1999. www.mtv.com.

25. Quoted in Judie Glave, "Jennifer Lopez," *Associated Press, Monday P.M. Edition*, July 19, 1999.

Chapter 5: A Star Is Born . . . Again

26. Quoted in Fleming, "Jennifer Lopez," p. 60.

27. Quoted in John Hiscock, "Jennifer Lopez—Highs 'N Lo's," *Mirror*, May 4, 2002, p. 33.

28. Quoted in Fleming, "Jennifer Lopez," p. 60.

29. Quoted in Degen Pener, "From Here to Divanity," *Entertainment Weekly*, October 9, 1998, p. 28.

30. Quoted in Fleming, "Jennifer Lopez," p. 59.

31. Jennifer Lopez, interview by Oprah Winfrey, *Oprah Winfrey Show*, ABC, May 17, 2002.

Chapter 6: Love at Last

32. Quoted in Pogrebin, "What Jennifer Lopez Really Wants," p. 74.

33. Quoted in Kaylin, "The Goddess," p. 250.

34. Lopez, *Oprah Winfrey Show.*

35. Quoted in Amy Longsdorf, "More Than Enough," *Bergen Record,* May 23, 2002, p. F07.

36. Quoted in Barrett Hooper, "There's J.Lo and There's Jennifer: But Don't Expect to Meet Both of Them at Once," *National Post,* December 13, 2002, p. PM6.

37. Lopez, *Primetime Live.*

38. Quoted in James Patrick Herman, "J.Lo on a High," *In Style,* January 2003, p. 154.

39. Quoted in Herman, "J.Lo on a High," p. 154.

Important Dates in the Life of Jennifer Lopez

1970

Jennifer Lopez is born on July 24 in Bronx, New York, to David and Guadalupe Lopez.

1975

Takes her first dance class.

1986

Appears in a bit part in the film *My Little Girl.*

1990

Auditions to be a Fly Girl on Fox television comedy show *In Living Color* but is rejected.

1991

Is accepted as a Fly Girl and moves to Los Angeles.

1993

Stars in short-lived series *South Central.* Appears in Janet Jackson video.

1994

Stars in two more short-lived TV series, *Second Chances* and *Hotel Malibu.*

1995

Makes her major motion picture debut in Gregory Nava's period drama *Mi Familia.* Beats out actresses Lauren Holly and Ashley Judd for a role in Francis Ford Coppola's *Jack.*

1997

Stars in *Selena,* becomes overnight star. Marries Ojani Noa.

1998

Stars with George Clooney in *Out of Sight*. Divorces Ojani Noa.

1999

Releases debut album *On the 6*. Begins publicly dating Sean "Puff Daddy" Combs.

2000

Wears scandalous dress to the Grammys. Stars in psychological thriller *The Cell*.

2001

Releases album *J.Lo* and stars in the movie *The Wedding Planner* at the same time. Both go to No. 1. Breaks up with Combs. Marries Cris Judd.

2002

Divorces Cris Judd, becomes engaged to Ben Affleck. Releases new album *This Is Me . . . Then*. Stars in *Enough* and *Maid In Manhattan*.

2003

Stars in *Gigli*.

2004

Stars in *Jersey Girl*.

For Further Reading

Books

Trevor Baker, *Jennifer Lopez*. London: Carlton Books, 2001. This young adult book contains a brief overview of Lopez's life and loves. It also includes several color photos.

Patricia J. Duncan, *Jennifer Lopez*. New York: St. Martin's Press, 1999. This young adult book contains a wealth of information about Lopez's early life. It is also translated into Spanish. There are a few black-and-white photos of Lopez in her early career, up to the release of *On the 6* in 1999.

Websites

Abstracts (www.abstracts.net). Detailed site with news and links to news about Lopez and other stars.

Entertainment Tonight (www.etonline.com). Website for the television celebrity–news show *Entertainment Tonight*. The link cited contains an interview with Lopez on the set of *Enough*.

Eonline (www.eonline.com). Website for celebrity news and gossip.

Jennifer Lopez Official Site (www.jenniferlopez.com). Lopez's official site for news, biography, and tour dates.

MTV (www.mtv.com). News and interactive site dedicated to the MTV network. Also contains a biography and articles about Lopez.

Teen Scene Magazine (www.teenscenemag.com). Teen site featuring archived Lopez news and interviews.

Works Consulted

Periodicals

Anthony Bozza, "Jennifer the Conquerer," *Rolling Stone*, February 15, 2001.

G. Brown, "Strike Up the Brand," *Denver Post*, November 25, 2002.

Michael Fleming, "Jennifer Lopez," *Playboy*, September 2000.

Judie Glave, "Jennifer Lopez," *Associated Press Monday PM. Edition*, July 19, 1999.

Sarah Gristwood, "Mouth of the Border," *Guardian*, November 20, 1998.

James Patrick Herman, "J.Lo on a High," *In Style*, January 2003.

John Hiscock, "Jennifer Lopez–Highs 'N Lo's," *Mirror*, May 4, 2002.

Lynette Holloway, "Keeping J.Lo in the Spotlight Has Risks for Her Career As Well As Rich Rewards," *New York Times*, December 9, 2002.

Barrett Hooper, "There's J.Lo and There's Jennifer: But Don't Expect to Meet Both of Them at Once," *National Post*, December 13, 2002.

Barney Hoskyns, "Jennifer Lopez," *Interview*, April 1997.

Chrissy Iley, "Lopez Lets Loose," *Harpers Bazaar*, December 2002.

Lucy Kaylin, "The Goddess," *GQ*, December 2002.

Ellen Lieberman, "On the Town with J.Lo," *In Style*, July 2002.

Amy Longsdorf, "Blood, Sweat and Tears," *Allentown Morning Call,* February 25, 1997.

——, "More Than Enough," *Bergen Record,* May 23, 2002.

Prairie Miller, "Selena Interview with Jennifer Lopez," *Ethnic News Search,* July 27, 1998.

Laura Morgan, "Livin' La Vida Lopez," *Seventeen,* January 2001.

Degen Pener, "From Here to Divanity," *Entertainment Weekly,* October 9, 1998.

Robin Pogrebin, "What Jennifer Lopez Really Wants," *Ladies Home Journal,* January 2003.

Stephen Rebello, "The Wow," *Movieline,* February 1998.

Rene Rodriguez, "From Fly Girl to Femme Fatale," *Miami Herald,* June 24, 1998.

San Francisco Examiner, "Jennifer Lopez: Take Me As I Am," April 10, 1997.

Sandy Sharpe, "Q the Interview: Jennifer Lopez," *Independent on Sunday,* December 1, 2001.

Megan Turner, "Jennifer's Big Cell," *New York Post,* August 13, 2000.

Mal Vincent, "Lopez Is Bursting into Hollywood Spotlight," *Virginian-Pilot,* March 22, 1997.

Bruce Westbrook, "A Tough Act to Follow," *Sunday,* July 28, 1996.

——, "Driven, but Not a Diva," *Chicago Tribune,* January 31, 2001.

Kevin Williams, "Lopez Says New Movie Has a Message," *New Pittsburgh Courier,* May 29, 2002.

Television Shows

Jennifer Lopez. Interview by Matt Lauer. *Today Show.* NBC, December 6, 2002.

———. Interview by Matt Lauer. *Today Show.* NBC, June 1, 1999.

———. Interview by Mark McEwan. *CBS This Morning.* CBS, March 21, 1997.

———. Interview by Mark McEwan. *CBS This Morning.* CBS, September 30, 1998.

———. Interview by Diane Sawyer. *Primetime Live.* ABC, November 13, 2002.

———. Interview by Oprah Winfrey. *Oprah Winfrey Show.* ABC, May 17, 2002.

Index

Picture Credits

About the Author

Heidi Hurst is an experienced teen magazine editor who has worked at *SuperTeen* and *M*. Now she is executive editor of *Tiger Beat* and *BOP*. She is also the author of Lucent Books's People in the News: *Britney Spears*. She is a Missouri native and graduated from the University of Missouri School of Journalism. She currently lives in Los Angeles.